"

By 2029 computers
will achieve human
levels of intelligence

– Ray Kurzweil

"

Published by
PHD
Fitzroy House
11 Chenies Street
London
WC1E 7EY

www.phdmedia.com

First published 2017

Copyright ©
PHD Worldwide

Author
PHD

Co-authors
Ben Samuel
Chris Stephenson
Elda Choucair
Holger Thalheimer
Malcolm Devoy
Mark Bowling
Mark Holden
Patrick Jeffrey
Phil Rowley
Rob Young
Toby Roberts
Wayne Bishop
Will Wiseman

Contributors
Angus Bannerman
Fabian Preiss
Faith Lim
Ian Dolan
Mark Coad
Matt Prentis
Oscar Dorda
Phil Hewitt
Rohan Tambyrajah
Simon Bird

With thanks to
Avril Canavan
Vicky Bloyce
Sara Barakat
Melissa Brookes

Design
Mark Vaile

The closing gap

MERGE

between technology and us

phd

FOREWORD

The onset of the 21st century is an era in which the very nature of what it means to be human is both enriched and challenged, as our species breaks the shackles of its genetic legacy, and achieves inconceivable heights of intelligence, material progress and longevity.

The price-performance and capacity of information technology are growing exponentially, generally doubling every year. The paradigm shift rate (the rate of technological progress) is also doubling every decade, which means in the 21st century we won't experience 100 years of progress – we will experience 20,000 years of progress at the year 2000 rate. By 2029 computers will achieve human levels of intelligence. This is not going to be an invasion to compete with us and displace us. We have already begun to merge with the intelligent technologies that we are creating. Ever since we picked up a stick to reach a higher branch, we have used our tools to extend our reach, both physically and mentally. The fact that we can take a device out of our pocket today and access virtually all human knowledge with a few keystrokes extends who we are. The smartphone in your pocket is a million times less expensive yet a thousand times more powerful than the computer all students and professors shared at MIT when I went there in 1965. That's a billion fold increase in price-performance in the last 50 years. And we will do it again in the next 25 years. What used to fit in a building now fits in your pocket. And what now fits in your pocket will fit inside a blood cell in 25 years, and will be far more powerful.

Within 20 years we will be able to send intelligent nanobots – blood cell-sized robots – into our bloodstream to keep our biological bodies healthy at the cellular and molecular level. They will go into our brains non-invasively through the capillaries to provide wireless communication between our neocortical modules and the cloud in the same way that your smartphone today extends its capabilities through wireless communication with the cloud. Our thinking will then become a hybrid of biological and non-biological thinking. So rather than competing with super intelligent machines, we will merge with them. As a result we will become smarter, more musical, funnier, etc. We will be able to back up our mind files, indefinitely extending the existence of our minds.

This is not as futuristic as it may sound. Today, Parkinson's patients have a pea-sized computer in their bodies with a connection directly into their brains that allows them to download new software to this computer from outside the patient. There are already blood cell-sized devices that can cure type 1 diabetes in animals or detect and destroy cancer cells in the bloodstream. These technologies will be a billion times more powerful in 25 years because their price-performance and capacity is doubling in less than a year.

While the social and philosophical ramifications of these changes will be profound, and the threats they pose considerable, we will ultimately merge with our machines, live indefinitely, and be a billion times more intelligent all within the next three decades.

———

Ray Kurzweil
Inventor, author and futurist

the best person I know at predicting the future of artificial intelligence

– Bill Gates

INTRODUCTION

THE HUMAN·TECHNOLOGY MERGE

Humans can perform tricks today that illusionists couldn't have imagined 50 years ago. Armed only with a tiny device that fits into our pockets, we can access a lifetime's worth of information in an instant; speak to anyone in the world whenever we choose; and share our experiences with friends thousands of miles away.

Schoolchildren can put on a virtual reality headset and journey to continents that previously took years for explorers to reach. Students can use a laptop to access billions of times more knowledge than the most prestigious university library could ever hold. Retirees can open a browser and be more informed on world affairs than the President of the United States was 20 years ago.

But the most astounding part of this technological trickery is the speed at which these new opportunities and experiences are emerging.

In the early 1950s, only a handful of computers existed. These machines were the size of a small room, weighed almost a ton and cost the equivalent of $4m (adjusted for inflation). Sales of the first mass-produced computer – the Universal Automatic Computer (UNIVAC) – totaled 46 units.

A few decades later, when mobile phones became commercially available, they weighed over a kilogram and cost thousands of dollars. Anyone lucky enough to own one of these bricks had to charge it for 10 hours to have a half-hour conversation.

Only a few people in any given area could use the network at the same time – any more calls and it would collapse under the pressure.

Any sufficiently
advanced
technology is
indistinguishable
from magic

– Arthur C. Clarke

Even in the early 1990s – less than 30 years ago – there were only 10 million people in the world with access to the internet. The web was a pet project at the CERN scientific research centre in Switzerland. There were no commercial search engines, browsers or apps and the concept of the smartphone was a distant dream in the heads of a few business visionaries.

Fast-forward to today and the progress is almost unbelievable. The humble computer's performance has increased one-trillion-fold and it is now in billions of homes across the globe. The world's cheapest computer, the Raspberry Pi Zero, weighs nine grams and costs $5. The smartphone in your pocket is more powerful than the computers NASA used to put Neil Armstrong on the moon.

Connectivity has increased from 10 million people to more than 3 billion. Mobile subscriptions outnumber the earth's population. Our computers, phones, cars, watches and homes are linked up to the web. Climbers on the summit of Mount Everest can take advantage of a superfast 4G connection. Sailors in submarines can use high-speed internet to call home. Astronauts can log-on to the web aboard the International Space Station, as it orbits the earth hundreds of miles up in the sky.

Fasten Your Seatbelts

This mind-boggling pace of evolution has taken us from a world without screens to one dominated by devices in just over 50 years. But this rapid evolution shows no signs of slowing down. In fact, it's speeding up.

Ray Kurzweil, Google's director of engineering, and one of the world's most respected futurists, puts this down to The Law of Accelerating Returns. Technology, he claims, isn't evolving in a linear manner (i.e. 1, 2, 3, 4, 5), it's instead advancing at an exponential rate (e.g. 1, 2, 4, 8, 16). This growth pattern has already been popularized by Moore's Law, which correctly predicted that the number of transistors capable of fitting onto a chip would double every two years. But Kurzweil believes this isn't only applicable to electrical circuits – it has a wider significance.

"It is not the case that we will experience 100 years of progress in the 21st century," he wrote in an essay, "rather, we will witness on the order of twenty thousand years of progress." In other words, because of this exponential growth, advancements made in the next couple of decades will multiply so quickly that they will dwarf the developments of the entire 20th century – a period that brought us the motor car, the airplane, the television, antibiotics, the PC, the internet and nuclear power.

Kurzweil's Law of Accelerating Returns isn't, of course, a universal law of physics – and some scientists oppose his thinking. Yet if even a fraction of this progress does materialize, then it means we are on the cusp of the most dramatic expansion of technology in history.

Some of these developments can be predicted without much consideration. Over the next decade, another four billion people will come online, doubling the number of users on the web. Connectivity will also spread to more devices. It won't only be our screens that link up to the web, it'll be almost every object we own. In fact, market intelligence firm IDC predicts that 80 billion devices will be connected to the internet by 2025, compared with 11 billion today.

Other potential areas of development are starting to emerge. Secretive companies like Magic Leap are working on mixed reality glasses that could turn the world into a digital canvas. Tech giants like Microsoft and Apple are creating virtual assistants that could soon become our digital PAs, automating our schedules and organizing our lives. Exciting startups like Helix are working on the next generation of personalized apps, based on our DNA.

But most of the innovation we'll experience is still incredibly hard to predict. How will the maturation of the field of nanotechnology impact us? What will society look like when we figure out how to connect our brains to the cloud? And how will governments legislate against the next 30 years of technological improvements? Few of us could have predicted the growth of smartphones in the 1980s, and the same is true today when trying to predict what might be coming over the horizon.

One thing's for sure, though: every successful technological breakthrough of the past has helped to unshackle us from a specific constraint – whether it's the physical constraint of only being in one place at a time, or the emotional constraint of not being able to communicate with loved ones. And, looking to the future, it is highly likely that humans will continue to use technology as a liberating force – as something that can help free them from all sorts of day-to-day constraints. This idea, combined with financial considerations (i.e. will this tech make any money?) can be used as a framework to help predict which technologies will take hold and which ones won't fly.

Closing the Gap

Another aspect of the future that we can confidently predict is our relationship with technology. Many of us today are heavily reliant on our devices. We spend more time staring at screens than we do outside, with friends or eating. Our smartphones rarely leave our sides. And as we move into the 2020s, our desire to be perpetually online will continue to grow. We'll find ourselves in a world in which we are as dependent on connectivity as we are on the oxygen we breathe.

How we access the web may change. Phones may turn into smart glasses. Glasses may turn into contact lenses. Contact lenses may turn into biological implants. But whatever form this tech takes, the goal will be the same: to keep us connected each second of the day.

As we spend an increasing amount of time in the virtual world, machines will become even more embedded in our lives. Technology sometimes already feels like it has its own mind – its own consciousness – but over the next two decades, this will become more pronounced. Machines will become as intelligent as us and, as this gap continues to close, we'll reach a point where we become indistinguishable from one another. Technology and humanity will – both symbolically and literally – fuse together.

We call this The Merge.

This journey has already begun and takes the form of five, clearly definable stages. In this book, we'll explore these phases, and assess how each one is moving us one step further along the path to convergence. In **Stage I**, we look at the early parts of the journey. We assess how specific innovations led to the commercialization of personal computers, and how the dawn of the internet enabled us to surface information in a revolutionary way. We also investigate how this has spawned a new era of marketing that laid the foundations for one of the most significant shifts the industry has ever experienced.

In **Stage II**, we highlight the three key inventions that led to the spread of the modern-day web. These giant leaps forward enabled us to organize the information we had surfaced, making it globally accessible

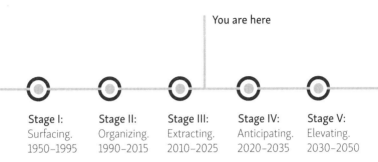

You are here

Stage I:
Surfacing.
1950–1995

Stage II:
Organizing.
1990–2015

Stage III:
Extracting.
2010–2025

Stage IV:
Anticipating.
2020–2035

Stage V:
Elevating.
2030–2050

and universally valuable. These inventions also helped create a portable device that brought us closer to our technology than ever before: the smartphone.

Stage III – the period in which we currently find ourselves – plays a pivotal role in The Merge. On the one hand, this era represents a maturation of the modern-day web. Search engines are smarter than ever, mobile penetration is widespread and connectivity is fast and reliable in many parts of the world. But then add dramatic developments in machine learning to this equation and a new phase entirely emerges. One where we're not just organizing information, we're also extracting new meaning from it – via operating systems, semantic search and cognitive assistants.

It isn't until the early 2020s that these exciting new ideas begin to have a major impact. In **Stage IV**, with the maturation of deep learning AI, technology starts to understand us, our context, our routines and it even starts to run our lives for us. Our assistants are by our sides constantly, helping us tackle all kinds of general tasks, not just specific things. They can anticipate our needs and desires, which in turn impacts how brands go about attracting our attention.

By **Stage V**, the final phase of The Merge, we have grown so dependent on technologies that the boundaries between the two have completely blurred. Artificial General Intelligence changes the way that we engage with day-to-day reality, sentient technology overlays our virtual existence onto the real world, and biological breakthroughs give us unprecedented control over our bodies and minds. Nanobots travel through our bloodstream, neural lace uploads thoughts to the cloud and brain-to-brain communication takes off. The human experience is elevated.

As these play out, our relationship with technology will change irreversibly. People will stop regarding machines as a separate entity – an "us" versus "them" mentality popularized by Hollywood and science fiction. Instead, the conversation will slowly shift. Technology will be regarded as an additional lobe of our brain – an essential and constant element in our lives on earth. The idea of "logging on" or "accessing the internet" will disappear – replaced by a constant connection in a world where the web flows like electricity.

"In the grand scheme of things, we do have many risks and challenges, but there is nothing else that matters more to the human race than this merger," says Bryan Johnson, a Silicon Valley CEO. "This is going to define how we evolve."

Be Prepared

This new world also threatens to overhaul modern marketing as we know it. Many decisions will start to become automated, brands will find themselves trying to influence an algorithm rather than a human, and breakthroughs in both hardware and software will generate new expectation levels in convenience and customer experience.

Merge is by no means an exhaustive list of the technologies that will shape our future. Instead, it focuses on specific advances that are likely to impact how people interact with brands. The book establishes the urgent implications for our industry and offers guidance on how to confront these challenges head on. It also shines a light on how marketers can assert influence by taking advantage of the transformational technologies of our time. Most importantly, it explains what needs to be done today to prepare for tomorrow – a world in which humans and technology become inextricably linked.

Let The Merge begin.

> **There is nothing that matters more to the human race than this merger. This is going to define how we evolve.**

SURFACING

STAGE I

1950 – 1995

The introduction and early spread of screens and the World Wide Web surfaces up information for us.

Every so often, a technology comes along that completely transforms the world. Two and a half million years ago, the early humans learnt how to fashion basic tools from stone. This changed how they prepared food and paved the way for more complex and functional implements – like cleavers and axes.

Two thousand years ago, the Romans discovered that mixing volcanic dust with pieces of rock and lime created a revolutionary new building material: concrete. This enabled them to construct architectural wonders – such as beautifully-arched aqueducts and huge amphitheatres – many of which still stand to this day.

Six hundred years ago, Johannes Gutenberg helped disseminate knowledge to millions of people in Western Europe by inventing the printing press. The machine reproduced books quicker and much cheaper than traditional handwriting techniques. Literacy rates soared and a new, modern era of history began.

Since then, a range of breakthroughs have changed society in different ways, from the steam engine to the airplane, the light bulb to the telephone. But it's only within the last 60 years that the latest technological transformation – computing – has begun. Today, nearly four billion people rely on screens to live their lives. They're in our homes, on our desks and in our pockets. And they're all built with one major objective in mind: to help us surface information whenever we want, wherever we are.

Those who can imagine anything can create the impossible

– Alan Turing

War Machines

The earliest computers, built in the 1940s, weren't conceived to help spread knowledge; they were designed as secret weapons in the ongoing war effort. The Harvard Mark I, built by IBM in 1944, was used by The Manhattan Project to assist with calculations for the first atomic bomb. The Electronic Numerical Integrator and Computer (ENIAC), built around the same time, was financed by the US army and was initially designed to calculate artillery firing tables.

Over the pond, a team working at Bletchley Park in the UK invented a machine called Colossus, which could decipher teleprinter messages intercepted from the German army. This went on to produce some of the most important intelligence breakthroughs in the Second World War. Today, Colossus is remembered as the world's first fully electronic computer. Its creator – Alan Turing – is known as the father of computer science.

In the 1950s, spurred on by advances during the war, this technology began to spread. The UNIVAC I launched in 1951, weighed 7.3 metric tons and was the size of a small apartment. It cost around $1.5m, making it a viable purchase only for government departments and big businesses. Among its first clients were the US Census Bureau, the US Navy and General Electric.

Over the next two decades, screens really began to proliferate. The introduction of color televisions meant they soon became a standard household appliance throughout the world. And a series of innovations in computing (transistors, integrated circuits, etc.) made these devices smaller, more powerful and less expensive – but they also turned computers into a truly global industry. In the late 1980s, for example, Japan owned 50 percent of the global semiconductor market and produced 80 percent of all SRAM memory chips.

Crucially, these innovations helped to open up these devices to much larger audiences. The Apple II, built by Steve Wozniak and Steve Jobs in 1977, cost $1,298 and quickly became commonplace in many US secondary schools. IBM's Personal Computer (PC) launched four years later and aimed to change perceptions of the devices from corporate luxuries to things that everyone should aspire to own.

This message quickly took hold. *Byte* magazine reports that 40,000 orders were made for the PC on the day it was announced. IBM had hoped to sell 250,000 computers over a five-year period – instead the company shifted three times that amount within the first two years. But, despite finding a new audience, these machines in the early 1980s were still little more than flashy typewriters. They had basic black screens with green text and required complex commands to perform simple tasks. In other words, they weren't accessible enough.

The User Revolution

In 1984, this changed overnight with the launch of Apple's Macintosh. It had a radical new design that looked, sounded and felt more intuitive to people who weren't computer enthusiasts. A graphical user interface (GUI) replaced the dull black screens and did away with the complicated command prompts. Users could simply navigate between icons and windows by moving a mouse in their hands. Calculators, alarm clocks and notepad applications on screen looked just like they did in the real world.

Many of these exciting new features had existed before the Mac's launch. The GUI first appeared in a computer called the Xerox Alto. The mouse was borrowed from Apple's previous model – the $10,000 Lisa. But the Mac's success lay in packaging these features into an easy-to-use and affordable home computer, one that felt like a friendly companion rather than a complicated and specialized machine.

In fact, Apple was so keen to emphasize the human-like qualities of the Mac that the company even programmed it to converse with the audience at the grand unveiling. "We've done a lot of talking about Macintosh recently, but today, for the first time ever, I'd like to let Macintosh speak for itself," said Jobs on stage at Cupertino's Flint Center of Performing Arts. He then walked over to the computer, clicked a button and smiled as it said: "Hello, I'm Macintosh, it sure is great to get out of that bag" – to rapturous applause.

By 1987, Apple had sold a million units. People were using the computers for everything from education to entertainment, finances to fine art. And the GUI, popularized by the Mac, went on to become the standard way that people interacted with screens. In fact, a couple of years after this launch, Microsoft's Bill Gates updated his MS-DOS software to Windows – a program that had a very similar look and feel to the Macintosh. Jobs and Apple considered this to be such blatant plagiarism that they launched a $5.5bn court case against Microsoft that rumbled on for four years. In the end, Microsoft emerged victorious – the court sided with Gates and Windows gradually became the dominant software used throughout the world. By the end of 1995, 100 million computers were powered by Microsoft's GUI.

But, in spite of this, the Mac's influence still lives on to this day in desktop computers, laptops, and even in smartphones. "I think the first Macintosh was like the Model T Ford – even 25 years later, you can see the resemblance to it," said Steve Wozniak in a 2009 interview with The Guardian. "Sure, one is a little bit cruder and simpler... but 20 years from now, we'll look at a Macintosh and pretty much understand the similarities."

Spinning the Web

Around the same time that IBM and Apple were introducing computers to new audiences, a scientist called Tim Berners-Lee started to wonder why there wasn't an easier way to access digital information on computers. He was working at CERN, the nuclear research facility in Switzerland, and became frustrated because many of the documents he needed to do his job were kept on separate machines – accessing them sometimes required learning an entirely new software program. "Often it was just easier to go and ask people when they were having coffee," he said in a 2015 interview with The Telegraph.

In 1989, Berners-Lee set out to make this information readily available to CERN employees, so people didn't have to jump through hoops to retrieve it. He wrote a proposal for a "large hypertext database with typed links" – a framework he believed would help to solve his problem. A year later, he had built the tools that now underpin the World Wide Web, such as HTML, HTTP and the original web server, as well as the world's first website: info.cern.ch.

As we all know, this novel way of uploading and sharing information quickly spread beyond CERN's research centre. By the end of 1993, there were 623 websites in existence. Two years later, there were 23,500 live sites, covering a variety of human interests: from business-based journalism on Bloomberg.com to one of the first online communities called – and we're not making this up – Bianca's Smut Shack.

Another website, HotWired, launched in October 1994 and was one of the earliest commercial online magazines. For obvious reasons, HotWired couldn't rely on print sales to generate revenue, so it quickly had to find a new way of funding its business. The team at the magazine therefore experimented with selling clickable ads that could be displayed on its site, adjacent to the editorial content.

The first of these "banner ads" – as they became known – was sold to AT&T for around $30,000. It consisted of a black box with the words "Have you ever clicked your mouse right here...You will" written inside. People who did click on the message were taken to a map on AT&T's website. This featured links to some of the world's best museums, like the Louvre in Paris – which were designed to show people how the web could transport them to exciting new locations from the comfort of their homes. Other sites quickly followed HotWired's example and took advantage of this new revenue stream. Vibe magazine, for example, signed deals with Timex, General Motors and Jim Beam.

Fast-forward to today and these early experiments have turned into a Goliath of an industry. Digital display ad spending is now worth over $32bn in the US alone, according to eMarketer. But HotWired's original banner will always occupy a special place in the internet's history, especially considering that it achieved a 44 percent click-through rate – an astounding figure when compared to today's average of around 0.05 percent.

Virtuous Circles

While often maligned as being ineffective and interruptive, online advertising played a leading role in helping to fuel the exponential growth of the web in the early 1990s. It quickly became a go-to business model for media companies and online publishers intent on following Sir Tim Berners-Lee's vision of an open, free web. In fact, a virtuous circle soon emerged: the growth of the web encouraged more people to buy computers, which in turn brought more people online, which in turn attracted more advertisers.

This unique combination – rapidly advancing computing power, the explosive growth of the web and the development of an early ad format – created the framework that would support the dramatic organizational progress made in Stage II. A phase that witnessed the birth of remarkable technologies that would go on to fundamentally change the world.

ORGAN|Z|NG

1990 – 2015

STAGE II

The organization of information through search engines, browsers, operating systems and apps helps us get to what we want.

———

The year 1995 will always be remembered as a breakthrough year for technology. It gave us the PlayStation, GPS navigation and the DVD. A site called AuctionWeb sold its first item – a broken laser pointer – before later rebranding as eBay. Sun Microsystems created a programming language called JavaScript, which went on to build a billion websites. And Microsoft's famous Windows 95 sold one million copies in its first four days of release.

In July 1995, a new kind of online bookshop sold and shipped its first item – in a sign of things to come, a textbook on artificial intelligence. Since then, Amazon.com has grown into a retail leviathan, shipping over one billion items last Christmas alone.

And that same year, two students called Sergey Brin and Larry Page first met. Brin, a graduate from the University of Michigan, was considering Stanford for his computer science PhD and was shown around campus by Page. The pair went on to build Google – a company worth over $500bn that's also the most valuable brand in the world, according to consultancy Brand Finance.

But, despite these landmark moments, in 1995 the digital world was still in its infancy. While tens of millions of people owned a computer, there were fewer than 24,000 websites in existence and only one percent of the earth's population was online. Even those with access had to use a modem to physically dial up to the internet whenever they wanted to use it.

Software is
eating the world

– Marc Andreessen

Screens were continuing to become cheaper, faster and more useful. TVs were now a truly global appliance, commonplace in homes throughout the world. Cable and satellite networks beamed hundreds of channels into people's living rooms. Information was spreading. But, in order to grow the web from a privileged luxury into a global utility, it had to become a) even more widespread and b) catalogued in a way that everyone could understand. Put simply, it needed to become better organized.

A Window onto the World

The first piece to this puzzle was the web browser, which helped users read the wealth of information online in a simpler, more effectively presented way.

Sir Tim Berners-Lee created the world's first browser while at CERN in 1990, and a whole host of early efforts – such as Cello, Lynx, Erwise and VoilaWWW – soon followed. But it wasn't until a young software engineer called Marc Andreessen invented Mosaic that the commercial browser started to gain widespread popularity.

Mosaic had a few key features that separated it from other browsers: it worked on all operating systems; it was easy to install; and it had a multimedia interface. So, instead of displaying lines of text with image links that users had to download, it displayed text, images and sound in the same window. This richer browsing experience made Mosaic a more attractive proposition to those without technical knowledge of the web. It became, according to CERN scientists James Gillies and Robert Cailliau, "the spark that lit the web's explosive growth."

By 1996, Andreessen had created a more advanced browser called Netscape Navigator, which commanded an 86 percent share of the market. It was the go-to tool for anyone wanting to read information in the easiest and most aesthetically pleasing way available. But Microsoft, which only had a 10 percent share of the market in 1996, quickly mounted a challenge to Netscape's supremacy. The company realized that packaging its browser in with Windows 95 could open it up to huge new audiences. By 1999, this strategy had worked and Microsoft had won the "browser war". Internet Explorer now owned a 99 percent share of the market and Netscape had been all but eradicated.

The invention and popularization of these browsers gave us a simple (and free) way of reading information on the web. And today's leading products – such as Google Chrome, Microsoft Edge and China's Qihoo – are all still built for that same purpose, albeit with much more advanced capabilities.

Needle in a Haystack

In the mid 1990s, buoyed by the popularization of the browser, the web grew at an incredible rate. In June 1994, there were just over 2,700 sites online. Two years later, that figure had risen to around 230,000. This variety made the web a richer resource, but it also meant that navigating all this information had become complex and often confusing. So, the second piece to this puzzle was in managing the diversity of the web – people needed to be able to find the information they were looking for, and fast.

A host of companies tried to solve this problem (remember Ask Jeeves, AltaVista or Lycos?), but it was, of course, Google that cracked the nut and changed everything. The company was officially founded in 1998 with a simple but incredibly ambitious mission: "to organize the world's information and make it universally accessible and useful." Google wasn't early to the game, but it approached the challenge from a completely different perspective.

Early search engines were more like directories: a giant list of websites where people could use keywords to search. But Google's secret ingredient was PageRank, a way of categorizing the web that graded pages based on relevance and popularity, not just keywords. This system uses bots (or "spiders") to crawl the web and analyze each webpage. In particular, the spider evaluates the number of other sites that link to that particular page. If a site has many links, the bots will rank it higher than one with fewer links. Other considerations, like how trustworthy the site is, are then combined to generate a unique PageRank.

This new approach created a highly accurate search engine that could help people find a needle in a haystack, in an instant. Google monetized the idea when, in 2000, it launched AdWords. This service allowed companies to purchase advertising space based on specific keyword searches. "AdWords offers the most technologically advanced features available, enabling any advertiser to quickly design a flexible program that best fits its online marketing goals and budget," wrote Google's CEO Larry Page in the launch release.

AdWords had instant appeal, which was largely down to two reasons: it allowed advertisers to only appear in relevant searches, where there was a higher likelihood of receiving traction; and it opened up the web to all companies, not just brands with big marketing budgets. A one-person business operating in a niche sector could purchase keywords that were specific to its area of expertise, rather than having to adopt the established broadcast interruption model.

In 2000, Google processed 20 million searches a day – providing plenty of options for the majority of brands to piggyback on with AdWords. Today, the search engine handles 3.5 billion searches every day and ad revenue exceeds $70bn per year. Advertising, powered by AdWords, has underpinned Google's success and has opened up new ways for the company to pursue its mission of making knowledge universally organized and accessible.

In the years after the launch of AdWords, Google's spiders continued categorizing sites. But the company also began uploading new content as well – growing the web, not just organizing it. Books, manuscripts and photos from the past were all scanned and digitized. A partnership with the British Library, for example, resulted in a chunk of the institution's archive (40 million pages, to be precise) being uploaded on to Google and made available to anyone with an internet connection.

In the past 15 years, Google has continued to grow the web by mapping cities, photographing streets and recording Earth from space. "Now Google is a global archive storing our history as it is made," wrote former employee, Miriam Rivera, on Entrepreneur.com. "It is as though a virtual world is being created right alongside our real world, a simulation of reality that grows more robust by the day."

A Mental Crutch

By bringing our world online, Google has forever changed how we go about our daily lives. We can now find any piece of information on the web, whenever we choose to. But we can also travel to any address, see landmarks from space and read ancient manuscripts. This has generated a reliance on technology like never before. Google has become our mental crutch, helping us access information without having to think or engage our memory.

In fact, two social psychologists called Daniel Wegner and Adrian Ward found that search engines have started to replace our memory as the primary knowledge bank – something they call The Google Effect. "When we are faced with requests for information we do not know, our first impulse is to think of the internet – our all-knowing "friend" that can provide this information to us after a simple tap of the finger," they wrote in the magazine *Scientific American*. "As we off-load responsibility...to the internet, we may be replacing other potential transactive memory partners – friends, family members and other human experts – with our ever-present connection to a seemingly omniscient digital cloud."

The Google Effect suggests that this reliance isn't just changing how we access information; it's also impacting how our brains function. And this effect is likely becoming more pronounced as ways of retrieving knowledge on the web become quicker and more frictionless. The smartphone, for example, has effectively put Google within reach 24/7.

Pocket Supercomputers

In the early 2000s, mobile phones were becoming commonplace throughout the world. In 2005, there were 2.2 billion subscriptions globally – an increase of over 2,500 percent in a decade. Smartphones (such as the Blackberry and PalmPilot) were also taking off, but tended to be luxuries afforded to business people needing to access their email on the go.

In 2007 – and for the second time in 30 years – Apple released a device that altered the status quo. "Every once in a while a revolutionary new product comes along that changes everything," said Steve Jobs at the iPhone's launch. This device wasn't the first smartphone. But, just like The Mac in 1984, it was the first to generate mass-market appeal – creating the template that helped these pocket supercomputers spread to billions of people.

In every aspect, the iPhone was a game changer, helping to considerably deepen the relationship between us and our technology. It didn't just give us another way of accessing the web, it provided an "always-on" connection to the internet. For the first time ever, we could take advantage of this online world whenever we pleased. 3G connections gave us the ability to surf the web on the go, so we could read the news, check our mail and chat with friends whenever we liked and wherever we wanted.

Smartphones also helped us interact with technology in a more humanlike manner. TVs had already become intuitive, as HD boxes from companies such as Sky enabled people to interact with these screens in an immersive way. But smartphones took this up another notch (or three). Gestures became commonplace, so instead of navigating information with a mouse and a keyboard (or a TV remote), we could pinch the screen to zoom in or out, or use our thumbs to scroll through information. These interactions immediately felt more natural, and much more user-friendly. Babies and young children could pick up the devices and understand the interface immediately. No technological knowledge was required.

As a result, smartphones quickly became the most important objects in our lives. "This is the fastest adoption of communication technology the world has ever seen," says Sheryl Sandberg, Facebook's chief operating officer. "What they do for our lives is transformative. They change how we access information, they change how we work, how we shop, how we live. And they keep us connected to other people on a day-to-day, minute-by-minute basis in a way that no other technology ever has."

Today, a handful of manufacturers are responsible for more than two billion smartphones worldwide. These range from Apple in the US, to Samsung in South Korea, HTC in Taiwan and OnePlus and Xiaomi in China. These devices are the first thing we look at when we wake up and the last thing we check before we go to bed. During the day, they never leave our sides. And the launch of Apple's App Store in 2008 gave them yet more skills. They're now our alarm clocks, cameras, diaries, sat-navs, stopwatches, camcorders, calculators and sources of entertainment. They have, in effect, become the remote controls of our lives – things we can use for almost any task in any given situation.

A Digital Limb

By 2010 – towards the end of Stage II – the App Store had celebrated its three billionth download and other stores, like Android Market (later renamed Google Play Store) were also enjoying rapid growth. In China, following Google's decision to exit the country, hundreds of different Android alternatives launched – many of which still exist today. Apps had become the killer software, transforming the mobile telephone from something primarily designed to make calls (with a few additional features) to something that could perform any task (and also make calls). DIY experts could use digital spirit levels to hang pictures correctly, athletes could map their runs with Nike+ and bored commuters could play games like Angry Birds.

The incredible utility of the smartphone deepened our reliance on these devices – and on tech in general. "This relationship with technology wouldn't have changed nearly as much if we were still sitting with laptop or desktop computers," says Larry Rosen, a professor at California State University. "Not only are we now carrying a computer in our pockets, but we're reminded of it 24/7." In fact, our love of this humble device intensified so fast that research from intelligence company Delvv found that one in three Americans would rather give up sex for three months than go without their beloved smartphone for just one week.

This research epitomizes how quickly and deeply people began to rely on screens. During this era, computing transformed from a rudimentary tool that some people used to surface knowledge to an organized world of abundant information. People could find anything with search engines and read it via browsers or apps. The online world began to feel like the third lobe of our brain. And smartphones – the defining technology of Stage II – became an extension of our existing bodies: a new, digital limb.

EXTRACTING

The introduction of machine learning leads to dramatic improvements in the extraction of information – from advanced operating systems and the semantic web through to virtual assistants.

The incredible rate of technological progression between 1990 and 2015 created a world where more than two billion people had access to the web. But it also produced an important side effect – one that would go on to define the next stage of The Merge – data. "There were five exabytes of information created by the entire world between the dawn of civilization and 2003," said Google's chairman, Eric Schmidt, at a conference in 2010. "Now that same amount is created every two days."

Since Schmidt said this, the volume of data being produced globally has again increased exponentially – and this is down to two main factors. Firstly, the number of people accessing the web has continued to rise. In 2010, there were just over two billion people online. By 2020, that figure will have doubled to four billion. By 2025, everyone will be online and superfast 5G networks will be pervasive. More people online means more searches conducted, more videos viewed and more items purchased – all of which creates more data.

The second factor is that entirely new streams of data have also emerged. The smartphone – which is becoming a truly ubiquitous device, with Ericsson predicting 6.1 billion people will own one by the end of the decade – has turned us into walking, talking data points. Sensors in these devices can track our location, map our journeys and

Whoever has the
best algorithms and
the most data, wins

– Professor Pedro Domingos

pinpoint which shops we visit. We don't have to "be online" to produce data any more – we do it every second of the day.

Connecting Everything

It's not only smartphones that are responsible for these new data streams. The emergence of wearables also help people record information, such as the steps they take, the miles they run, number of calories they burn and even their heart rate throughout the day and night. Most of these devices are wristbands – such as the Apple Watch, Xiaomi Mi Band and Fitbit – but as the space evolves, new designs are also cropping up. Motiv, for example, manufactures a smart ring that responds to gestures and measures fitness levels 24/7.

More specialized trackers can help patients remotely record other data points, such as their blood pressure or skin temperature, without having to visit a surgery or hospital. A startup called Echo Labs, for example, is working on a wearable that can analyze vital signs in the wearer's bloodstream to give a deeper indication of their health. The device uses optical sensors and spectrometry to measure respiratory rate and oxygen levels – effectively turning arteries into flowing streams of data.

"The commoditization of these devices is lighting up data, which was always there, but was previously invisible or inaccessible," says Dave Coplin, Microsoft's principal tech evangelist. "The interesting thing here is that I've always had a heart rate, but now this is visible and creates a data stream that I can leverage to change my behavior."

In addition to wearables, other inanimate objects have also been brought online. Mercedes now manufactures connected cars, Withings produces smart scales, LG makes connected TVs and L'Oréal has even created a connected hairbrush. There are smart ovens, washing machines, fridges, doorbells, thermostats, photo frames and plant pots – yes, plant pots.

This connected world even extends to the workplace. Some companies are already fitting their employees with wearables that track their sleep, emotional state and interactions with other people. Consulting firm Deloitte, for example, has experimented with giving members of staff "sociometric badges" that contain a microphone and accelerometers to monitor movement. "Within five years, every company ID badge is going to have these sensors," says Ben Waber, CEO of people analytics company Humanyze, which makes the badges. "Ten years down the road, you'll start to see the sensors also integrated into the clothes you wear."

The increasing popularity of these smart objects, combined with the ubiquity of smartphones, is creating an ultra-connected era. Machina Research predicts there will be 27 billion smart products by 2025, a huge increase from just over six billion in 2015. In this new world, we no longer have to access the internet via a screen. Our homes, our clothes, our cars and even our bodies are being hooked up to the web. And every object – whether it's a toothbrush or a car – is generating its own stream of data.

At the beginning of Stage III, however, many companies didn't know how to take advantage of this data flood. A study by the International Data Corporation (IDC) found that, of the 2.8 trillion gigabytes of data that had been created by 2012, only 0.5 percent were actually being used. The behavioral economist Dan Ariely perhaps summed it up best when he tweeted: "Big Data is like teenage sex: everyone talks about it, nobody really knows how to do it, everyone thinks everyone else is doing it, so everyone claims they are doing it."

A Giant Leap Forward

However, as this stage has matured, technologies have emerged that help us extract meaning from data much more effectively. The most important of these breakthroughs is machine learning (ML) – a generalistic term referring to algorithms that can achieve certain goals by being fed huge sets of information. There are many kinds of ML, but one of the most impactful methods has been something called "supervised learning", in which a computer is trained up by "reading" vast amounts of labeled data and learning from it.

ML is not a particularly new invention. Its origins can be traced as far back as Stage I. "The fundamental mathematical ideas around machine learning had been worked out before 2010," says Greg Corrado, a senior research scientist at Google and one of the co-founders of the Google Brain Team. "This all started in the 1950s, but the most important ideas were established in the 1980s and 1990s."

So why is it so significant now? Corrado compares the rapid improvements in ML at the beginning of Stage III to the quest for flight in the late 19th century. In the 1890s, he says, many people were trying to build machines that could fly, with little luck. But at the turn of the century, this suddenly became feasible because people realized that the limiting factor had been the weight of the internal combustion engine – it was too heavy for airplanes to get off the ground. As soon as people designed lighter engines, air travel took off.

"Flying went from being possible to being relatively commonplace in a decade, and the same thing happened with machine learning," he says. In this instance, though, the breakthrough was cheap computation. "If you're only allowed to swing your hammer three times, you're not going to learn to make new things – that's basically what slow computation was," he says. Cheap, fast computation has given people the opportunity to tinker, to play around, to experiment and to iterate rapidly. "It's the difference between a space where there's tremendous innovation and a space that's dead," Corrado adds.

This convergence – of available data and affordable computational power – has created a machine learning gold rush. ML has rapidly morphed from a discipline that scientists studied in universities to something that companies are investing in heavily. In particular, seven companies are leading the charge: Google, Microsoft, Facebook, Apple, Amazon, IBM and Chinese search company Baidu. These firms have all opened secretive research laboratories and are frenetically mopping up top AI talent from around the world – the Google Brain Team, for example, has expanded from three members in 2011 to over 100 members in 2017.

Seeing is Believing

ML has provided a more powerful way of extracting meaning from data – helping us make massive advances in specific areas of technology. Advances that, just a few years earlier, would have felt more like science fiction than an imminent reality.

One of the best examples of this progress is the field of machine vision – getting computers to "see" like we can. Accurately recognizing what's in a photograph may seem like a simple task, but it's a skill that has eluded computers for half a century. When shown images of things that are different, but look similar – like Chihuahuas and blueberry muffins or sleeping puppies and bagels (if this sounds crazy, just Google it) – computers have historically struggled to differentiate between the two.

"After 50 years of work, computer vision systems could [identify images correctly] 72 percent of the time. The consensus was that there were decades more work before this would properly start working," said Benedict Evans of VC firm Andreessen Horowitz, in a recent presentation. "Then, in 2012, machine learning started working and everything changed." The error rate of computers dropped from 28 percent to just 7 percent. By the end of Stage III, that will be closer to 1 percent.

This incredible progress is down to a supervised learning algorithm called a neural net. These nets consist of many layers of nodes and are loosely based on the neurons in the human brain. The nodes, like our neurons, aren't particularly smart on their own, but collectively they can achieve incredibly complex tasks. "These deep neural networks have lit up the data we already had in an exciting new way," says Microsoft's Dave Coplin. "They've taken us to places that we could only have dreamt of before."

The ability to differentiate between dogs and baked goods might seem like a novelty achievement, but it has paved the way for giant leaps forward in machine vision. Artificial intelligence (AI) software developed by the University of Oxford, for example, can now watch videos of people speaking and correctly identify what they are saying 93 percent of the time. LipNet, backed by Alphabet, is significantly more accurate than human lip-reading experts, who tend to know what a person is saying between 20 and 60 percent of the time.

Stanford researchers have also used a neural net to identify cancer from photos of people's skin. The team fed 130,000 images into an algorithm and then used it to differentiate between malignant and benign skin lesions. "Today, AI can diagnose melanoma on the skin of someone who lives in a village without electricity at the same rate of correct diagnosis as someone in the best clinic in the UK," says Sheryl Sandberg, Facebook's chief operating officer. "Now that's incredible."

Sandberg's company, Facebook, is also using machine vision to improve the lives of 250 million visually impaired people around the world. The Automatic Alternate Text program, which launched in 2016, can identify images posted in someone's News Feed and dictate a description to a user. So, if someone posts a photo of a birthday cake along with the message: "best day ever", the program recites the message and then explains there is a cake in the accompanying photo. In 2017, this software was updated to interpret actions, as well as objects. So instead of just saying "cake", the algorithm can understand when someone is "cutting a cake" or "blowing out candles on a cake".

Soon, this service will become much more advanced. "Our goal is to enable even more immersive experiences that allow users to 'see' a photo by swiping their finger across an image and having the system describe the content they're touching," wrote Piotr Dollar, a scientist at Facebook's AI Research lab in a blog post. "Our next challenge will be to apply these techniques to video, where objects are moving, interacting and changing over time." Ultimately, the team wants visually impaired people to be able to experience a live broadcast.

If Facebook can recognize what's in any image, then it can use this for several other purposes too. In February 2017, the company announced that its machine vision neural net, called Lumos, is now powering search across Facebook. This enables people to find images by using keywords – so typing "beach" should bring up photos of your recent holiday. The company has also used its object recognition technology to analyze the characteristics of 160,000 people in the US who posted photos of cats or dogs. The public study found that "cat people" are more likely to enjoy sci-fi films, less likely to be in a relationship and have 26 fewer friends on average than "dog people".

In the next few years, this functionality could even go on to impact the way brands advertise on the platform. Facebook could, for example, create fresh audience insights by exploring the images that people post. Are they into sports? Do they have a pet? Are they always drinking coffee? The company hasn't indicated that this is in the pipeline – but with an estimated two billion photos uploaded to Instagram, WhatsApp, Facebook and Messenger every day – it easily holds enough data to make this useful for the three million advertisers using the platform.

I Hear You

Similar advances are being made in speech recognition. Back in 1952, Bell Laboratories in the US created a transcription tool that recognized human speech. The device only distinguished between 10 numbers, but was considered a breakthrough at the time. By the 1990s, commercial transcription services were available and could recognize continuous speech at around 100 words per minute. By 2001, the technology had reached 80 percent accuracy.

But just like machine vision, speech recognition plateaued throughout Stage II. Companies struggled to make any kind of significant improvements to the accuracy of the technology until ML capabilities became more advanced around 2010. Fast-forward to today and Baidu's system has a 96 percent accuracy rate in speech recognition. Apple and Google are not far behind, with a 95 percent and 92 percent accuracy rate respectively.

The importance of these improvements is huge. Take Google's translation service. This initially launched in 2006 and, over the next decade, grew a userbase of 500 million daily users. It supported 103 languages and translated roughly 140 billion words every day. Then, in September 2016, Google changed the algorithm that powered its translation service to a neural net called Google Neural Machine Translation (GNMT) – developed by Corrado and the Google Brain Team. Within a matter of days, the platform made bigger improvements than the old system had managed in 10 years. It evolved from something that sort of worked in some languages (but for others was pretty much unusable) to something that suddenly became highly useful in many languages.

"These systems can now translate a sentence that is unlike any sentence they have ever seen before," says Corrado. "The old translation system operated at the level of phrases, this new system operates at the level of whole sentences. This starts to feel like a qualitatively different experience. It was science fiction just 10 years ago." In fact, Corrado believes that, if you extrapolate that progress into the future, then you really begin to see a transformational experience. "I believe that in the next few years, it will get to the point where if you want to have a conversation with someone whose preferred language or mother tongue is different from your own, it's something that's seamless and easily available on your own phone."

Brain Bots

These advances in machine learning – in particular, speech recognition and machine vision – have paved the way for a new wave of technologies that are starting to make a genuine impression on people's lives.

At the most basic level, ML-powered chatbots are being integrated into platforms to automate conversations between brands and customers.

ARE WE FALLING IN LOVE WITH TECHNOLOGY?

As Stage III evolves, our reliance on technology will continue to grow. It will become our assistant, our right-hand man, our omnipresent helper. But could we ever take this relationship a step further? Could we ever fall in love with our technology?

This idea has already been explored on the silver screen. Spike Jonze's 2013 film *Her* told the story of a man who – having just endured a broken marriage – falls for a virtual assistant called Samantha. The intuitive operating system is accessed via a "hearable", and gradually wins over the affection of the movie's main character, Theodore Twombly.

In the real world, too, there are early signs that some people might be entering in to an emotional relationship with AI. In 2015, Microsoft in China launched a chatbot called Xiaoice that was designed to mimic the personality of a teenage girl. The OS quickly gained more than 40 million users and a massive 25 percent of them said "I love you" to the assistant.

In neighboring Japan, there's even a name for this phenomenon. "One reason for the lack of babies is the emergence of a new breed of Japanese men, the otaku, who love manga, anime and computers – and sometimes show little interest in sex," wrote BBC journalist Anita Rani in 2013. A key driver behind this "otaku" sub-culture is the popularity of a

Nintendo game called Love Plus, in which people take their virtual girlfriend or boyfriend on dates and talk with them whenever they choose.

A number of people have become so emotionally attached that they've vowed never to end the relationship – suggesting it's more than a passing fad or a Tamagotchi-like game.

And in the UK, a virtual assistant called Robin is receiving more and more sexually explicit questions, according to the company's CEO. The VPA was originally designed to give traffic advice and offer directions to truckers, but many users are also treating her more like a girlfriend than a piece of tech. "This happens because people are lonely and bored.... It is a symptom of our society," said Ilya Eckstein, chief executive of Robin Labs, in an interview with *The Times*. "As well as the people who want to talk dirty, there are men who want a deeper sort of relationship or companionship."

So, if there are already trappings of human-technology relationships, how might these evolve in Stages IV and V? Advances in virtual reality and mixed reality will make the idea of a virtual partner far more vivid. Searches on Google for "VR porn", for example, have increased by 9,900 percent between 2014 and 2016. So, couple the immersive and realistic experiences of VR with the rise of virtual worlds (such as those being built by Improbable) and the foundations are there for much more lifelike human-tech experiences.

It's surely not a future that will be explored by everyone, but how might it impact society if this becomes more popular and socially-accepted throughout the world?

The technology first took off when Facebook announced it was opening its API on Messenger in April 2016, which essentially made it simple for any developer to build a chatbot for the service. By September that year, over 30,000 bots had been created for Facebook Messenger, including the 1-800-Flowers bot (which automated flower delivery); the Hello Hipmunk bot (which offered travel advice) and the Domino's bot (which let people order pizza without speaking to a human). Other platforms, such as Kik, Slack and Skype, launched similar stores the same year.

"Bots are an opportunity to incorporate AI into processes that bring people and businesses closer together," says Sheryl Sandberg. "They help to get things done and they do it fast. It's really early but we see a lot of potential for brands in terms of engagement, awareness, retention, commerce and customer service."

Sandberg cites Estée Lauder's bot that works on Facebook Messenger as an example of their potential. To accompany the launch of its pop-up shop in London, the beauty brand built an accompanying chatbot that let people buy products and have them delivered by instant courier in under an hour. "All aspects of commerce were handled in Messenger without customers needing to access other digital channels, and because it's a bot, it's fast," she adds. "I think people really appreciate that."

But, while some bots have nailed the customer experience already, most others are still too dumb to answer simple questions. Facebook's VP of messaging products, David Marcus, admitted late last year that the first bots on Messenger were "really bad". However, considering the rapidity of progress that ML has made in fields such as translation and image recognition, it would be foolish to bet against them quickly becoming usable on a mass scale. Research from Oracle, for instance, found that 80 percent of business leaders planned to implement chatbots by 2020. "Where we're heading in the very short term is, if you don't have a chatbot, then you're not open for business," says Microsoft's Dave Coplin.

As chatbots become more accurate over the next couple of years, they'll start to become essential business tools. They'll turbo-charge any brand's customer service channels by offering an instantaneous support network that never sleeps, never needs a lunch break and never has a bad day. "Within five years we'll all be interfacing with digital employees on a daily basis – both as customers and as co-workers," says Daniela Zuin, marketing director at IPsoft, a company that builds cognitive bots. "Agents will be able to understand me, diagnose what I want and even follow guidelines to figure out what needs to happen next."

Out of home (OOH) experiences will also become powered by bots. Already, a Japanese canned coffee brand called Georgia has linked its vending machines to the chatbot in its mobile app. So, when registered customers are in the machine's vicinity, they'll receive a message from the bot saying: "Good morning" or "What a blue sky today". These greetings also become personalized to individuals, so if someone visits the machine to have their second coffee of the day, the bot might say: "Rough day?" or "Hey sport, don't overdo it". This concept first launched in 2014, and early results were positive – over 68 percent of people interacting with the machine felt a more personal connection to the brand. It is therefore easy to see how this kind of interaction could spread to other OOH experiences in the future – effectively creating a ubiquitous cognitive layer across multiple touchpoints.

Knowledge Management Blockchain

This will put pressure on organizations to bring together all of the information about their product/service – the ingredients, processes, supply-chain partners, etc. It is quite possible that this will be the most significant usage of blockchain technology – a collective of connected knowledge of every organization that is constantly being updated. A supplier changes something about how they operate and it automatically impacts all other connected businesses.

At Your Service

Another breed of bot – virtual personal assistants (VPAs) – is also making huge progress thanks to the capabilities of Stage III ML. Just like chatbots, VPAs are underpinned by natural language processing and speech recognition technologies. But, unlike chatbots, they are designed to answer any questions or commands asked of them, not just specific ones. A useful assistant should be able to schedule a reminder, look up the football scores, check tomorrow's weather forecast – and do pretty much anything in between. "I really feel like virtual assistants are the holy grail for technology companies today," says Microsoft's Coplin. "Because in a sense, they are the ultimate interface."

The most widespread VPAs are smartphone assistants, and these first emerged towards the beginning of Stage III. Apple launched Siri back in 2011, Microsoft followed suit in 2014 with Cortana and Google joined the party in 2016 with Google Assistant. Early in 2017, Samsung announced that its Galaxy S8 handset will come with an integrated assistant called Bixby, powered by a company called Viv (which was set up by one of Siri's founders – Dag Kittlaus – and was acquired by Samsung in late 2016).

These smartphone-based VPAs aim to provide a more intuitive way for us all to interact with our devices. Research by Nokia, for instance, found that people currently check their phones 150 times per day. But being able to talk naturally to a VPA removes this distraction. Rather than unlocking your phone, opening an app and typing into a screen, users can simply talk to Siri, or Cortana, or Bixby and make it do the heavy lifting for them. It's not a viable solution for every situation (you might not want to talk to your VPA while on a bus or in a library) but in certain environments it has the potential to remove several layers of friction.

Fulfilling this ambition, however, is incredibly tricky. "Humans can transform our thoughts into the common currency of language effortlessly. All the context, grammar, syntax and connotation is bundled up seamlessly and we don't have to think about it," says Google's Greg Corrado. "Getting machines to do these things – to understand what a sentence means, or even have the suspicion of what a sentence means – has proven to be dramatically difficult."

Today, VPAs are being used by millions of people on a daily basis to answer basic questions or perform simple tasks. But transforming them from nice-to-have tools to genuine "assistants" – capable of helping us with more complex problems – requires two key steps.

Firstly, the tech must become more reliable. ML has already brought natural language processing and voice recognition on leaps and bounds, but there is still some way to go. "People underestimate the difference between 95 percent accurate speech recognition and 99 percent," said Baidu's VP and chief scientist Andrew Ng at a recent conference. "It's an incremental four percent improvement but it's actually a gamechanger." Next-gen VPAs therefore require an accuracy rate of 98 percent or higher, which we haven't yet reached.

Secondly, companies building this technology need to cooperate more effectively with one another – putting the user first rather than trying to lock people into their ecosystem at the expense of other assistants. Siri, for example, has always worked with pre-installed apps but Apple didn't open its Application Programming Interface (API) to any third parties until recently. So, the VPA could search for something using Safari, but couldn't conduct the same search on Facebook or Twitter, or any app that Apple didn't own. This effectively turned VPAs into walled gardens: they worked within strict parameters but didn't encompass every platform and service on a smartphone.

Opening Up

Fortunately, this is now changing. At its Worldwide Developer Conference in 2016, Apple announced that it was finally allowing other companies to integrate its assistant into its products. You can now ask Siri to send a message on WhatsApp, make a payment on Square, call someone on Skype and map your exercise on Runtastic. In December 2016, Google and Microsoft announced they'd also open up their VPAs.

The true pioneer of these open and collaborative VPAs is, however, Amazon. In November 2014, the retail giant launched Echo: a cylindrical speaker with a built-in assistant called Alexa, which is designed to be placed in your home. At the time of launch, users could ask Alexa questions, add items to their Amazon shopping basket, play songs from Prime Music and get the latest news headlines or weather updates.

Three years later, the number of tasks Alexa can perform has skyrocketed. In February 2017, the device had over 10,000 registered "Skills" from third parties and was adding over 1,000 more every month. Users can request an Uber, adjust their Nest thermostat, post a message to Slack or order a coffee from Starbucks. Or they can receive help with household tasks, such as cooking. A Skill from the Jamie Oliver Group, for instance, lets people ask the celebrity chef for meal inspiration. Once they have settled on what they want to rustle up, the Skill emails them a list of required ingredients as well as the cooking instructions.

While Amazon doesn't release official sales figures for the Echo, it did admit that demand for the devices around Christmas 2016 was nine times higher than the previous year. A report from Consumer Intelligence Research Partners from November 2016 estimated that over five million of the devices have been sold in the US since launch.

And it's been tipped as "Amazon's next billion-dollar business" by numerous publications. The reason behind this excitement is simple – Echo does something for everyone.

For the consumer, it puts an assistant where they're spending a big chunk of their time – in the home. It doesn't rely on a screen, so if you are busy cooking then you don't need to wash your hands, dry them, unlock your phone and then speak your command. And, perhaps more importantly, it's easy and natural to converse with. Amazon is so laser-focused on providing a natural experience that it has recently updated Alexa with Speechcons – slang words that add emotion and nuance to the device's lexicon. Ask Alexa a question now and she may reply with "Bada bing", "Good Grief" or "Boom".

For third parties, it gives them an opportunity to interact with people in a new environment. Now, brands can reach people in their living rooms, kitchens or bedrooms. And if you're Campbell's Soup, or Uncle Ben's, or Lurpak, what better place to be than in someone's kitchen, when they are cooking?

And for Amazon, Echo has the potential to re-engineer the company's relationship with millions (or even billions) of people. Right now, Amazon is a straight-forward supplier. People come to Amazon.com, order the goods they want and the company fulfills the purchase. But Echo turns Amazon into a middleman that mediates every request, conversation and purchase between customers and thousands of brands. Echo could therefore become a gatekeeper, giving the company tremendous leverage and influence in the near future (more on that in Stage IV).

The phenomenal success of Amazon Echo has created a frenzy of activity from other tech giants, all eager to take advantage of this sudden interest in voice-powered devices. Google launched an Echo competitor – Google Home – in November 2016 and Apple is rumored to be working on a similar product. Chinese firm Beijing LingLing has created the DingDong – a device that looks, feels and has very similar functionalities to the Echo. And even toymaker Mattel has its own version, called Aristotle, which is designed to be placed in a kid's bedroom and acts as an assistant for both parents and kids.

It can be used as a baby monitor, read bedtime stories or sing lullabies, help with homework and even re-order things such as wet wipes or nappies on command.

Ambient AI

Devices like Echo have shown that, in the near future, VPAs will no longer exclusively live within a smartphone. They will leap out of the screen and start to embed themselves in all sorts of environments. A partnership between Amazon and Ford has already put Alexa into people's cars, for example. Echo owners can listen to audiobooks, play music from Spotify and add items to their Amazon cart while driving. Apple has recently added Siri to all its devices, so people can access the assistant on their laptops at the office, on their iPad at home or via their watch while jogging. The company's new Airpods – Bluetooth-connected earphones with a mini computer inside – also put Siri in your ears.

In fact, some experts are touting "hearables" as the most important growth area for virtual assistants over the next couple of years. "Since the early 1980s, human computer interaction has primarily been facilitated through Graphical User Interfaces (GUIs)," wrote Christine Todorovich, principal director at design firm frog in the company's 2017 Tech Trends report. "However, the combination of screen fatigue and technology embedded into everything is exposing a need for new types of interfaces that extend beyond the visual." Todorovich believes that "2017 will be the year of the AUI — the Audio User Interface."

In addition to Apple's Airpods, Sony has developed an in-ear device that lets users interact with a virtual assistant without looking at a screen. The Xperia Ear helps people check diary appointments, send messages (via dictation) and listen to social media updates on the move. Other products, like Doppler Labs' Here One earbuds, replace the "analogue" audio that you receive in your ear with a digital audio signal. They are smart enough to change ambient sounds that the user hears around them – so if they're on public transport and want to drown out a conversation happening nearby or laser in on a conversation that is happening across the room, they can do so easily. Intelligent VPAs are surely the next logical step for the company – they already have an integration with Siri – as is real-time translation. In fact, consulting firm Wifmore believes these "hearables" are such a rich area for innovation that, by 2018, the market could be worth $5bn.

But before the hearables market can truly take off, significant improvements must be made to the tech. The product needs to become less obtrusive, so you can forget that you are wearing it. And the battery life must also last at least a full day (currently Here One will only last

Stage III Technologies: Present and Future

1. Next-gen Wearables

The next wave of smartwatches to be independent of smartphones and have deep-view technology, so they can read blood, assess hydration, etc. The addition of smart rings with embedded microphones will lead to significant increase in engagement with VPAs.

2. Hearables

Companies such as Doppler Labs with its "Here One" product will create a new kind of device. Will be a carrier for the VPA and allow for location messaging and event experience augmentation.

8. First-gen MR

Magic Leap and Microsoft are likely to lead the way. Early products likely to have commercial adoption. As the price drops and portability increases, it will become a consumer device. This will enable an information layer to be overlaid onto the world.

7. The AR Web

Advancements in cloud computing will enable the creation of a universal environment that we all share. This will logically lead to the construction of parallel worlds – advertisers will create branded worlds, just as they currently create websites.

3. Next-gen VPA

The achievement of 98%+ accuracy level with true natural language and organic personality development will be a game changer. As will the result of a full, extensive open API network that will allow you to ask or buy anything.

4. Messenger Concierge

Conversation augmentation within messenger and video chat environments that add to the conversation with information and can organize and book for you.

6. Data Layer

An intelligence layer across all video content (leveraging machine visioning) will enable people to know about any object, place, and yes, brand. Social plug-ins will enable purchases. Video will emerge as a new retail channel.

5. NLUI Chatbots

Chatbots will include NLUI (Natural Language User Interface) to enable voice conversation. And they will appear as a layer across websites, display ads, apps and out-of-home experiences. The technology will enable people to intercept video ads and seamlessly engage with the characters in the ads.

two and a half hours). It's therefore more likely that the full adoption of hearables won't take place until the end of Stage III. But, when it does happen, the opportunities for marketing could be vast. For example, brands could "tether" audio information to a highly specific location, which would then fire up a message when the user passes by (subject to opt-ins). Walk past a book store and someone could hear a suggestion to buy the newly released book by a particular author that they have previously bought, for instance. If managed well, this could become a utility that we will adopt immediately – we'll even find it hard to remember what life was like before these messages.

Now We're Talking

The key question that remains is: how will we talk to our hearables? The developers claim to have ambient microphones embedded into them but that is unlikely to solve the privacy concerns for people who don't want to talk out loud, when other people are listening. Holding a smartphone to the mouth doesn't really solve this problem either, and it doesn't allow for an immediate response (as people would have to dig into their pockets or bags to retrieve their phones – hence creating a barrier).

The answer will most likely to come in the form of a ring. As mentioned earlier, wearable tech rings are about to become relatively commonplace – with Motiv being the most advanced product currently available. As well as carrying out the usual functions – heart monitoring, mobile payments, door-unlocking – the next generation of these devices are likely to have embedded microphones. This will become the perfect complement to the hearable device because it will provide an effortless way to respond to voice commands. It will also be more private – i.e. people could cover their mouth while speaking into the ring. If this way of communicating becomes a natural and culturally accepted action, then rings could prove to be a game changer in how we connect to our virtual assistants.

Listen Up

Whatever form these virtual assistants take – whether they're in your phone, in your ear, or even in a smart ring – they're likely to listen in to more and more conversations as Stage III evolves. Their goal? To know you better so they can become a "messenger concierge" – an assistant that can help you throughout the day with all sorts of administrative tasks. Already, Facebook's VPA (called M) can listen in and make recommendations based on conversations that are happening between two or more people in Messenger. So, if someone types "Where are you?" then the assistant might ask if you'd like to share your current location with them.

M Suggestions was initially rolled out to a select few users, but future developments could benefit brands in the near future. Could M, or indeed any other assistant, listen out for potential purchase moments in conversations? If someone asked their friend about how to remove a stain, for example, then surely that would be the perfect time for Vanish to serve up an ad? Or if a group of friends were chatting about what to do over the weekend, perhaps an ad for a local theme park or cinema could appear with a group booking discount code. This model would ensure that all ad suggestions made perfect sense within the context of the conversation, and could operate on a pay-per-click or even pay-per-conversion model – thus ensuring maximum return on investment.

The potential of this new advertising model is even greater with ambient AI devices that could listen to our conversations constantly, not just when we have an app open. Could, for example, Samsung know that you're interested in buying a new car and serve up relevant ads? Or could a hearable listen in to a conversation you had with a friend about a Picasso exhibition and then say: "There are still spaces left on Saturday, shall I book two tickets for you?"

This shift will also impact the way in which companies optimize information online. When users type on keyboards, they tend to prefer highly focused descriptions because entering information can be slow and cumbersome. However, people can usually speak much quicker than they can type, which fundamentally changes how they search. Instead of typing "seafood restaurant London", they're more likely to say "what are the best seafood restaurants in central London?". As this shift becomes more pronounced, brands will need to restructure their paid, owned and earned assets to ensure that queries answer a need state – "where", "how", "when" or "find me", "tell me", "get me" – rather than a written keyword. And, as answering these verbal articulations becomes more important, marketers will also have to start considering how their brand "sounds" as well as how it "looks".

Companies will also have to bear in mind that, as voice search proliferates, people will no longer see pages and pages of suggestions from a search engine. Today, if someone types a query into Google, they will see many suggestions and may click on any one of the top 10 results. But, if someone conducts the same search via voice, the assistant may only mention the top two options. The consideration set will therefore shrink considerably, meaning that the brands at the top of the ranking will continue to grow in influence – in other words, big brands will get bigger.

Ultimately, as we become used to having these helpers with us 24/7, speech will become the dominant way in which we extract information from the web. Already, one in five searches on Android are conducted by voice and ComScore estimates that this will reach 50 percent by 2020. "Looking to the future, the next big step will be for the very concept of the 'device' to fade away," wrote Google's CEO, Sundar Pichai, in a letter to his staff in late 2016. "Over time, the computer itself – whatever its form factor – will be an intelligent assistant helping you through your day. We'll move from a mobile first to an AI first world."

Mixing Realities

This doesn't mean that screens will completely disappear from our lives by the end of Stage III. But it does suggest that the form factor is likely to change – new devices that blend into our lives more seamlessly and don't require us to access the web through a five-inch piece of glass will become commonplace.

Smart glasses are one such device. Google was the first major company to create a product in this space when it launched Google Glass in 2012. This optical wear contained a tiny screen that could overlay information onto the real world to save people from checking their phones whenever they needed to use the web. Despite a huge amount of buzz, several factors meant that Google Glass didn't quite take off. The device was ugly, raised privacy concerns and was ultimately too expensive ($1,500) for widespread adoption.

But, five years later, the smart glasses space is heating up and most major tech companies are getting in on the action. South Korean giant Samsung, for example, debuted a set of mixed reality spectacles at the 2017 Mobile World Congress. The Monitorless glasses let users switch between VR and AR easily and are designed to work with a smartphone or computer – helping to make the content leap off the screen and into the real world. Chinese firm Baidu is also continuing to invest heavily in the AR space. And Apple is rumored to be working with lens specialist

Carl Zeiss on a headset of its own, expected to launch in late 2017 or 2018. In fact, UBS analyst Steven Milunovich claims that the brand has over 1,000 engineers working on augmented reality technology in its research centre in Herzliya, Israel.

And Facebook is also in the race. As announced at F8 2017 they have built powerful deep-learning AI that can understand the physical world as it moves – this will enable them to layer in mixed reality. This technology has been opened up to developers, but currently restricted to a camera. However, they are also developing glasses – but yet to produce anything.

Microsoft is currently leading the race, though. The company debuted HoloLens – a wireless headset that overlays high-definition holograms onto the surrounding environment – back in 2015. The device enables the wearer to interact with both the real world and virtual world simultaneously by using a selection of gestures and voice commands. It is currently only available commercially, but a consumer release is expected within the next couple of years.

The opportunity for brands to benefit from this technology is huge, and companies have already been experimenting with it. Volvo, for instance, has used the device to help car buyers visualize their ideal car in dealerships. The HoloLens enables the manufacturer to bring up a hologram of a virtual car and then seamlessly change the vehicle's features, such as the size of the rims or the color, and even strip-back the bodywork to see the chassis. The home improvement store Lowe's is also using HoloLens to help people build a bespoke kitchen. Customers can select their ideal appliances, surfaces and color palette and then put on the device to experience a virtual reconstruction of their design.

But, despite the early progress made by HoloLens, most people expect the smart glasses sector to really take off when a company based in South Florida enters the fray. Magic Leap has attracted investments of $1.4bn from the likes of Alphabet, Warner Bros and big-name VCs such as Andreessen Horowitz and Kleiner Perkins. Few people know what's going on behind closed doors, but most people who have seen the tech believe it could be a game changer. This is what David Ewalt – a Forbes tech journalist invited to the company's secretive headquarters, wrote after experiencing a demo in 2016:

"When it arrives – best guess is within the next 18 months – it could usher in a new era of computing, a next-generation interface we'll use for decades to come. This technology could affect every business that uses screens or computers and many that don't. It could kill the $120 billion market for flat-panel displays and shake the $1 trillion global consumer-electronics business to its core. The applications are profound. Throw out your PC, your laptop and your mobile phone, because the computing power you need will be in your glasses, and they can make a display appear anywhere, at any size you like."

Even if the company's first generation product doesn't meet the expectations of the hype, it's unlikely to deter investment because the potential for smart glasses is so vast. Grand View Research, for instance, predicts that mixed reality (MR) will be worth $6.8bn by 2024. "The goal is to make VR and AR what we all want it to be: glasses small enough to take anywhere, software that lets you experience anything, and technology that lets you interact with the virtual world just like you do with the physical one," wrote Mark Zuckerberg, Facebook's CEO, in a post in early 2017.

Blurring Boundaries

When these smart glasses do become commonplace, they'll completely blur the boundaries between the virtual and real worlds. We'll no longer have to experience the web through a screen. Instead, rich new environments offering a truly immersive and communal experience will be built. Marketers will finally stop building brand websites, and instead they will build brand worlds – environments that you can enter and explore and purchase.

In fact, a London startup called Improbable is already laying the foundations for this new era by building these next-gen experiences. The company recently partnered with Google to launch SpatialOS – an operating system based in the cloud that lets developers "build simulated worlds on a massive scale".

Right now, this new world is designed to create super-immersive and collaborative gaming experiences, where thousands of people can participate in the simulated reality. But Improbable is also creating a detailed simulation of an entire UK city. "The model, dubbed Improbable City, will combine systems like traffic patterns, energy consumption, waste management and other elements, to create the most advanced simulation environment of a city ever created," explained an article in Wired.

Once created, people will be able to use the model to determine how specific changes might impact actual cities. So, if traffic levels were to double in Improbable City, how would this impact the flow of citizens, for example? "We'll give you a world in a bottle that you can use to ask questions of the real world," said Improbable's founder, Herman Narula, in the same article.

As these new worlds are built, an AR-web will emerge in which simulated reality and actual reality blend together in high definition. Virtual cities, like Improbable City, will be overlaid onto existing environments, giving users the opportunity to control every pixel they see in front of their eyes. "We'll be able to modify reality and mix it with the virtual world in literally any way we want," said Michael Abrash, chief scientist at Oculus, in a recent presentation. "Any part of the scene could be virtual or real, and you could also mix the two closely." You could, for example, change colors or textures of surfaces as you please, or even build your own custom environment and then send it to anyone else to also experience.

A Wired World

This new environment, in which information is all around us and not just within a smartphone screen, relies on the convergence of many complex technologies. Mixed reality hardware needs to become smaller, more powerful and available at scale; the AR-web requires huge progress in both software capabilities and processing speeds; and ML-powered tools must become smarter and more intuitive so that we can control our experiences in a natural way. But, if these hurdles can be overcome, the results could be genuinely transformative. "With AR [and MR], you're not just replacing a screen with a simple visor, you're replacing a bad experience from a five-inch phone screen with a full wrap-around virtual world that's indistinguishable from the real thing," says Dr Ian Pearson, a futurologist.

As these macro shifts take place, a new "wired world" will emerge, where AI flows around us like electricity. Machines will have human-level senses, such as speech, hearing and sight. They'll respond to subtle gestures like the pinch of fingers or the bat of an eyelid. They'll become the third lobe of our brain as well as an extension of our nervous system. And, as ML continues to get smarter, our technology will start to do more than just improve the way we extract information from the world – it will also anticipate our needs, thoughts and movements.

And this is when things really start to change.

ANTICIPATING

2020 – 2035

STAGE IV

Deep learning AI leads to technologies that anticipate our needs and interests, and even start to make decisions for us.

———

In August 2016, a group of scientists published a paper in the *Journal of Oncology Practice* that offered an intriguing insight into the future. The team, from Microsoft Research and Columbia University, used anonymized data from the search engine Bing to predict early signs of pancreatic cancer – long before doctors could diagnose the disease.

To do this, the researchers first identified people who typed in diagnostic queries – i.e. "I have just been told I have pancreatic cancer". Then they examined that person's previous search history to isolate the earliest possible indication that they may have the disease. "When an individual who doesn't know they have cancer starts to research a few initial symptoms, this system could extrapolate that data and pick it up months before a typical diagnosis," says Dave Coplin, Microsoft's principal tech evangelist. "It was all done by looking at the patterns and making that semantic connection."

The experiment wasn't perfect – results pointed towards a 5 to 15 percent success rate – but ongoing improvements in the understanding and analysis of data should dramatically improve that percentage. The researchers concluded that "low-cost, high-coverage surveillance systems" could soon be deployed to passively observe online behavior and predict all sorts of cancers that are currently difficult to diagnose.

This future – where technology is employed by humans to help anticipate certain conditions, needs or desires – will define the next

Everything that we formerly electrified we will now cognitize

– Kevin Kelly

stage of The Merge: a phase where data isn't just used to extract meaning, but to predict eventualities with a high level of accuracy. Granted, this is already possible to a certain degree: Amazon uses ML to suggest what book you might like to buy next based on your past reading history; Google Now anticipates you'll leave work at 6:00 p.m. and informs you if the traffic is bad; and meteorologists can predict what the weather will be like this weekend (sometimes, at least). But, over the next decade, these models will become far more reliable and hyper-personalized to individuals. Tinder, for instance, is already working on pre-emptive dating, where the "Tinder Assistant" will arrange dates for you based on AI-driven intelligence.

As this takes hold, we will move from a society that uses generalistic predictions to one that revolves around highly accurate and informative calculations. One where technology knows what we're doing and what we might do next. A world that's cognified as well as connected. "AI turns prediction into a commodity," says Coplin. "It lets you predict things that were previously impossible, but also things you didn't even know were possible to predict."

Welcome to Stage IV: Anticipation.

Preventative Measures

This seismic shift is already starting to happen in healthcare, which is gradually transitioning from treating diseases to trying to proactively prevent them. And wearables, which IDTechEx Research predicts will be a $70bn market by 2025, will play a leading role in making this a reality. In Stage IV, these devices won't just count your steps and monitor your movement, they'll also track your vital signs and anticipate problems before you know anything is wrong.

Researchers from Stanford University's genetics department have already offered us a glimpse of this future. The team recently conducted an experiment where a group of 60 participants were asked to use up to eight wearable devices each. These monitored their weight, heart rate, oxygen levels, sleep patterns, skin temperature and steps taken (among other things) on a continuous basis. In total, nearly two billion measurements were recorded, which were then combined with additional tests conducted in the lab, such as blood samples.

Early findings indicated this data could predict the onset of illness days before the person felt any symptoms. For Michael Synder, a professor of genetics at Stanford and one of the participants, fluctuations like an increased heart rate and decrease in blood oxygen levels helped reveal the onset of four separate bouts of illness during the trial. Soon, he believes this prediction ability will be embedded into an app on people's smartphones. "For inflammatory illnesses, I think these sickness-predicting wearables will become more accurate and move from research to the consumer," he says. "I also think they will move to the early detection of other diseases, such as neurological and immunological conditions."

As this happens, there will be an increasing opportunity for brands to lend a helping hand. Early detection of a common cold could, for instance, provide a notification that you are about to get a cold and healthcare brands could then send you a cold-prevention spray. The same holds true for products like tissues, cough medicine or chicken soup. These ads would enable marketers to pay for media opportunities on a highly targeted basis, but any brands seeking to take advantage of this would have to do so in a sensitive and compassionate way – ensuring there is a fair value exchange so the consumer opts in.

But this opportunity isn't only limited to when people are falling ill. As sensors become more widely available, brands will use them to get a better idea of people's state of mind, as well as their tastes and interests. British Airways has already filed a patent application for a digital pill that could help the brand tailor its in-flight experience. Passengers could swallow the pill before they board and it would then "detect internal temperature, stomach acidity and other internal properties and wirelessly relay this information outside the passenger's body," according to the patent application. So, the airline crew could anticipate hydration levels and bring you a glass of coconut water, or a natural herbal relaxant if you are anxious. More importantly, the company could also use it to detect signs of deep vein thrombosis.

Perhaps the biggest health-related opportunity of all, however, lies in genome sequencing. This procedure, which can unlock vital information about an individual's biological composition by analyzing their DNA, was first carried out successfully in 2003. Since then, it's become far more accessible and affordable. In 2006, it would have cost around $14m to sequence a whole human genome. By 2015 that had reduced to $1,500 (and much cheaper, partial sequencing was also available) and by 2025, it could cost just a few cents – or it could be offered for free via an ad-funded model. This exponential decrease in price means that, within the next few years, both brands and consumers will be able to use genome sequencing in a whole new way.

Helix is one company that's driving this shift. The San Francisco-based personal genomics startup aims to let anyone simply and affordably sequence their DNA so they can discover new insights about their unique biological make-up. This, in turn, lets them make more meaningful decisions in areas such as health, nutrition and family planning. But, as well as offering genome sequencing, Helix is also inviting brands to develop services that help consumers act on these insights – kind of like a DNA App Store.

"We believe in providing an open platform where trusted brands and companies can develop and deliver products that can be used everyday by millions of people," says Robin Thurston, Helix's CEO. "For example, based on what your genetics can tell you about how you metabolize iron, a nutrition app could add more green leafy vegetables into your personalized meal plan." Or a fitness app, like Nike+, could access data about your genetic susceptibility to muscle tears and then create a tailored running regime so you don't injure yourself. "Personal genomics can help partners drive innovation, making much more personalized and relevant products and experiences, which will ultimately open the door for new business opportunities," Thurston adds.

Slicker Cities

Being better equipped to understand our bodies and anticipate health problems is likely to have a big impact on the overall quality of our lives. But it will also have a wider influence on society. As fewer people die each year from chronic diseases (largely due to preventative measures becoming effective), the global population will surge. The UN predicts that, by 2030, there will be 8.5 billion people in the world – an increase of 1.5 billion from 2017. That's roughly equivalent to the population of Zurich being born every day.

What's more, a report from Allianz predicts there will be 40 megacities by the end of Stage IV and the greater Shanghai area could even become the first "gigacity", with a population of up to 170 million inhabitants. "By 2030, two-thirds of the world's population will live in cities; many of them in megacities," said Allianz's chairman, Axel Theis, in the report. "The trends of tomorrow are being born in these cities and we will need to find answers to the enormous challenges they pose."

At the top of this list is figuring out how to make these cities smarter, so they can accommodate these vast populations. In Stage III, people's homes gradually became more intelligent as sensors brought inanimate objects online and Ambient AI began to flow freely. In Stage IV, the same will happen to entire urban areas. Street lights, bus stops, cars, bikes and buildings will become connected. Predictive maintenance – in which sensors alert councils to infrastructure problems (i.e. a damaged rail track) before problems arise – will become commonplace. And algorithms will be able to process masses of data in order to anticipate human movements throughout the built environment.

Chinese tech giant Baidu is already working on building these services. In 2014, a stampede during the New Year's Eve celebrations in Shanghai killed 36 people and injured a further 49. So a team of scientists at Baidu have set about creating an early-warning system that aggregates search data on Baidu maps in order to anticipate human movement around the city. The researchers also built an ML program that can process a variety of data inputs and measure the risk of potential crowd disasters. If a problem is likely to occur within the next one to three hours, it will notify the protective services.

"In the near future, machine learning will become more and more important in behavior research," says Haishan Wu, a senior data scientist at Baidu and one of the project's leaders. "Soon this will be used to predict human behavior in all aspects of life, ranging from crowd behavior to other forms of social and economic behavior."

In the US, researchers at MIT University are working on a different kind of prediction model – one that uses advanced machine visioning to anticipate "plausible futures of static images". The team fed two million images from Flickr into an algorithm, which was then tasked with generating short video clips showing what might happen next in each photo. For instance, an image of a beach triggered the system to create a clip of crashing waves. And a photo of a train at a station generated a video of the locomotive leaving the platform. "Predictive vision will enable artificial systems to anticipate human needs and patterns," says MIT's Carl Vondrick, who co-authored the paper. "It might anticipate a person's goal and complete it for them; or it could potentially predict hazards or accidents and attempt to prevent them."

The most obvious application for this technology is in driverless cars. Machine vision software could, for example, foresee the movements of other vehicles on the road and even anticipate when an accident is about to happen – taking preventative measures to avert the driver from danger. Volvo Trucks' 360 degree scanning technology can already monitor the movements of pedestrians, cars and cyclists in the near vicinity and warn the driver if someone is in their blind spot. But as the tech becomes more sophisticated, preventative measures will increasingly be taken autonomously based on prediction models, like the one devised by MIT.

Driving the Disruption

It's difficult to predict when fully autonomous vehicles will become commonplace, mainly because this relies on government legislation and infrastructural development as well as technological innovation. But when they do – sometime in Stage IV – they will have a massive impact on road safety. McKinsey estimates that up to 150,000 lives will be saved on US roads by 2025, simply by removing the possibility of human error.

They'll also make our journeys much easier and more streamlined via car-to-car communication. This technology, which is already being installed in premium models, enables the car on the road to "see" hazards and then warn other connected-cars in the vicinity. So, if there's an ambulance at the next junction, nearby cars will be alerted and can then take actions to ensure the journey isn't disrupted.

Autonomous vehicles will also free up people's time when they are behind the wheel. Instead of staring at the road, commuters will be able to work, host meetings, watch TV or even catch up on sleep. This, Morgan Stanley believes, will generate an additional $507bn in "productivity gains" in the US alone. Cars – like all other connected devices, will also become media channels, as people are now free to be interrupted by messages or lured in by tempting offers. And when these cars drop passengers off at their destinations, the vehicles will be able to park themselves in giant lots away from the crowded central business district. This will lead to less-congested cities, as cars no longer have to drive around the block to find a space and then park on the side of the street.

It's realistic to assume that, by 2035, this futuristic ideal could have taken shape. Uber, Lyft and Tesla will all control advanced networks of intelligent vehicles throughout many of the world's megacities. These companies will respond to customer demands in an even more seamless way than ride-sharing services today. People won't have to push a button for a ride – instead, their virtual assistant will share their calendar with the autonomous network of their choice. So, when someone's meeting finishes at 10:00 a.m., a car will be outside to whisk them to their 10:30 a.m. appointment. Or, if calendar information isn't available or their schedule changes, a simple command to their assistant ("Get me a car home now") will be all that's required to arrange near-instant transportation.

Bot Brokers

This seamless experience would require the network of autonomous vehicles to be widespread enough to deal with demand and respond to requests quickly (which is already the case in many large cities, albeit with driver-operated taxis). But it also relies on the maturation of next-gen VPAs – virtual personal assistants that have reached a 98 percent conversational accuracy rate (or higher) and have near human-level intelligence. These assistants would be completely personalized to you: they'd know your likes and dislikes, they'd understand your habits and they'd be able to use this information to automate complex tasks on your behalf.

Take organizing a holiday. Right now, booking a trip requires people to manually conduct research in a number of separate domains. They have to book flights, evaluate the best hotels, arrange transportation and explore potential activities. This creates an immediate barrier to the holiday-booking process. But in Stage IV, much of this could be handled by a next-gen VPA that can anticipate what you would do and act on your behalf. Microsoft's Dave Coplin describes this as follows:

"I could say to my assistant: 'I'd like to take my family to Canada in April,' and it would know who I am, it would know who my family are, it would know which airline I like to fly with, the hotels I like and the things I do in my spare time. So, on my behalf, it would negotiate with all of the service providers and present me with a completely curated experience. 'Dave, here is your holiday, shall I book it?'"

This may seem far-fetched considering the current abilities of VPAs and bots, but many of the major tech companies are already working on making this a reality. During 2016's Build Developer Conference, Skype's principal group program director, Lilian Rincon, showed how Microsoft Cortana could introduce various bots into Skype's next generation app to help streamline a booking process. In the live demo, Rincon opened up the Skype app and asked Cortana to block out her calendar for two days because she was planning to attend an event in Dublin. Having done this, Cortana then looped in the Westin Hotels bot (Rincon's hotel chain of choice) so that she could easily book a room without leaving the Skype conversation.

By Stage IV, VPAs will do much of the heavy lifting on administrative tasks and will then present us with the best options based on our interests and budget. And it won't just be booking hotels or organizing holidays: "Anything that follows a pattern is a prime target to be automated by an assistant," says Coplin. And, for decisions that matter less to us – like re-ordering cleaning products or re-stocking the pantry – our VPAs could even start to automate the decision-making process entirely. Our connected fridges, for example, will automatically monitor what's inside (using a combination of image recognition cameras and sensors) and will automatically re-order items as soon as they run out. The same goes for subscription services: a VPA could be alerted when someone uses their last razor blade, triggering it to request more blades from Dollar Shave Club.

This scenario could also apply to companies that offer a commoditized service, such as utility companies or even banks. A VPA could constantly scan all the available savings accounts on offer at any given time and seamlessly move someone's money to the service that provides the best interest rate. The same could happen with insurance, entertainment subscriptions, gas and electricity providers.

Accenture has already created a blockchain-based smart plug that can shop around for different energy suppliers to provide the best possible price to people as and when they need to use electricity. This, the company believes, could create a future where households can automatically alternate between energy providers under a new type of "smart contract". If someone was about to have a cup of tea, the connected kettle could negotiate the best price for electricity in the split second before it was boiled – always ensuring that the household got the best deal available at that particular moment in time.

Buy Before You Try

As people get used to virtual assistants making decisions on their behalf, they will even entrust them to start making speculative purchase decisions based on predictions about their needs and interests. So, if someone is hitting the gym more than usual (in January probably, because some things will never change), the assistant could proactively recognize that their body requires more energy than usual and could therefore order protein powder, chicken breasts and an extra pack of bananas. Or, if someone is trying to lose weight, the assistant could track their progress by connecting to their smart bathroom scales and then tailor the next day's grocery shop accordingly – fewer treats, more green veg.

In fact, Amazon has already patented this concept of "anticipatory shipping". Here, the company would use data about a particular customer to predict what they might want to buy next. Amazon would then ship these items to the sorting office closest to that person's house, so if they did hit "buy" the fulfillment process could happen quickly (possibly within an hour or two, by Amazon Prime Air, the company's drone delivery service). This service could even extend to shipping items without the customer ordering anything at all – Amazon could predict what people might want, or need, and deliver them on a speculative basis – if people didn't want an item, they could simply return it for a full refund.

This model has obvious advantages – it creates a delivery network that can facilitate orders quicker than ever, and locks people into the convenience of Amazon in a deeper way than before – but there are also some clear hurdles. What happens if the company interprets the data in the wrong way and delivers an insensitive item, such as sports equipment to someone who had just broken their leg, or a pet toy to a family whose dog had just been put down? Perhaps the company will just avoid this by only sending items deemed to be safe enough for anticipatory shipping – no one is going to get upset if an extra pack of kitchen roll arrives. Or perhaps the VPA could become the mediator, only signing off anticipatory deliveries when it deems them to be appropriate enough.

Marketing to Algorithms

Entrusting our VPAs to make decisions on our behalf doesn't mean that we will stop making decisions altogether. Rather, we will delegate our assistants and smart appliances to make the best choices for us in a number of low-interest categories, leaving us with more time to think about the things that matter to us. We'll concentrate on decisions like which car to buy or what clothes to wear. The decision-making process will also become increasingly immersive. So, someone will be able to put on a VR headset and compare a resort in Turkey to a villa in Portugal by "experiencing" them both beforehand. They'll also be able to walk into a shopping mall and use their mixed reality glasses to bring up additional information on the clothes that take their fancy – again to help them make the right choice about a purchase that means a lot to them.

A multi-tiered marketing ecosystem is therefore likely to emerge. At one end, emotional advertising will become increasingly important for high-interest categories, as they compete for our attention. Video ads will become more cinematic, with beautifully crafted and aesthetically shot films being shown. And as mentioned in the previous chapter, NLU-chatbots will also be embedded into the viewing experience, so people will be able to take action if an ad resonates with them. Experiential advertising will also become increasingly important, sucking the consumer into a memorable, highly-participative journey.

At the other end, low-interest brands will increasingly find themselves marketing to an algorithm, rather than a human. Customers will be less receptive to price offers or functional benefits because their VPA will be constantly monitoring these to ensure they always get the best deal. Instead, companies will have to understand how virtual assistants make purchase decisions and alter their strategies to meet this criterion. In effect, they will have to start marketing to an algorithm, as well as (or instead of) the human cerebral cortex.

It's hard to accurately predict how these algorithms will be programmed to make choices on our behalf. But factors such as past purchase history, budget and individual tastes are likely to play a leading role. Consumer reviews (which are used by many app-based services today) will become an increasingly important way for VPAs to differentiate between brands and make choices accordingly – especially in sectors where there are many similar products on sale, such as FMCG.

Brands must therefore place more emphasis on obtaining positive reviews from customers. Just like Uber and Airbnb currently ask people to review every trip, so too will beer brands, or canned food manufacturers in Stage IV. This could become part of their marketing strategy – for instance, digital out-of-home ads could encourage people to rate their experience of a particular product. Or, brands could incentivize customers to leave feedback by offering discounts on future purchases.

This review-based system will shift the key targeting moment from a pre-purchase nudge (buy this, buy this!) to a post-purchase feedback request (review this, review this!). In fact, some of the time we save making decisions on what to buy could be partly taken up with giving our virtual assistants constructive feedback on the product or service – thereby strengthening the feedback loop at every given stage. However, pre-purchase nudges won't disappear. Rather, marketers will have to become adept at predicting the routine ebb and flow of people's needs and interests so that they can pre-emptively market products to people before they even know they might want them. For example, a company might analyze someone's personalized tracking data to ascertain whether that person is about to enter a "purchase decision window" – i.e. to understand if someone might soon be open to considering that particular product or service.

But this combination of pre-purchase nudges and post-purchase reviews won't always be enough. Companies will also have to ensure they are sustainable and ethical enough to meet the VPA's exacting standards. Purposeful marketing has been one of the most influential marketing trends of recent times, as more and more people look to buy products and services from brands that proactively make a positive impression on the world. And in Stage IV, this will become seamlessly embedded in the purchase decision. An orange juice brand might score slightly lower in terms of taste and price, but if that company is also ensuring its supply chain is using renewable energy, that could tip the balance in its favor.

Knowledge Management

The deeper the AI can peer into companies and their supply chains, the greater the information it will have to make a decision. To that end, companies are likely to take knowledge management much more seriously. AI will help here. Every ingredient, process, or external company that influences the product or service will be captured and organized by AI, so that it can then be accessed by AI. This movement to improve knowledge management will start in Stage III and will help chatbots function more effectively. But it will be a necessity in Stage IV, when virtual assistants are making decisions based on this. It will also lead to a new level of transparency, beyond what we have currently experienced with the advent of the internet. And this, in turn, will compel organizations to improve their practices.

All brands must therefore make investments before Stage IV to clearly define their identity and build their core values around issues that genuinely matter to society. Doing so will position them favorably in the eyes of a decision-making virtual assistant. The one question that remains is: what are we going to do with all this free time? Will technology free us up and then leave us to our own devices (literally and figuratively)? Or will it want to play more of a role than simply create space for us? Perhaps it might even seek to elevate us – either physically, mentally or spiritually.

THE CHANGING ROLE OF THE AGENCY / MARKETING CONSULTANCY

By Stage IV, the agency/marketing consultancy will look very different.

Much of the work traditionally carried out by a planner will now be handled by machine learning and/or artificially intelligent reinforcement learning. A virtual personal assistant (VPA) will also handle many of the consumer's decisions, so the end user will often also be a machine. An agency model will therefore arise whereby, some of the time, machines are marketing to other machines.

In this model, the micro-decisions made by planners and buyers across digital channels will be replaced. Our algorithms will determine the creative message that should be displayed to a specific segment in a specific environment at a specific time of day. Thousands of decisions will be made every second – and these decisions will be made by AI.

We are still some way from this reality, and realising it will require attribution models and trading platforms to blend together. It will also require "true AI" (i.e. reinforcement learning algorithms) that can deal with incomplete datasets and the probabilistic nature of factoring in the long-term and indirect contribution of brand-based communication. But this will happen.

Marketing Technologists will be Prevalent

When most of the decision-making processes are made by machines, planners will instead focus on the construction and development of marketing technology. In other words, their roles will become even more important – and building this capability now is a priority.

Data Analysts Working with Cognitive Assistants

In addition to this, we will also require advanced data analysts. Ad and marketing technology will probably create a level playing field, but data will be a key differentiator between advertisers. Therefore, it will become (even more of) a competitive advantage. Data analysts will use cognitive assistants to interrogate the data – expanding audiences from seed data, segmenting that audience and then enriching it to find out more about them. Again, investing in this skillset is a priority today.

A New Breed of Cognitive Consultants

Beyond paid media, a cognitive layer will be built on top of websites, ads and apps (see Stage III), and this will result in new specialists. These teams will help clients generate new knowledge by pulling in a vast array of information about the company, products, ingredients and the supply chain into one database. Chatbots and VPAs will then "peer" into this data and will build a "cognitive layer" – enabling people to ask questions about the company. And then build this into all brand touchpoints – including creating video ads that people can interrupt with voice and ask questions of the characters within the ad and even continue the conversation through to a booking.

The Maturation and Segmentation of Ecommerce Expertise

Machine visioning will create information layers across video formats, and this will enable people to "tap and speak" to find out about any item, and purchase. In essence, video will become a retail platform. And, as both hearables and mixed reality (MR) devices become more popular, this information layer will eventually overlay onto the real world, not just video. People will be able to see anything, find out more information and buy.

Brands will therefore need to create layers of information within the right context. Then, they'll need to engage with the software that mediates that particular experience – in other words, they'll need to interact with an MR browser or a hearable operating system. Costs will be incurred on a "cost per action" basis – i.e. only as users decide to purchase something.

Ecommerce expertise will also be required for connecting to the VPAs – so that the brand is mentioned, or for some low-interest/commodity categories, automatically selected by the VPA.

These different ecommerce environments will have their own specialists, within the agency.

The New Role of the Strategist

With each of these increasingly specialist areas the role of the strategist will be more important. They will need to understand each of the different areas well enough so that they can steer clients.

With the increasing complexity, the strategist will know an increasing amount more than the marketing teams about what can be done. With this the role of the strategist is likely to move from that of selling a subjective worldview on the best way forward to advising based on a superior understanding on what is achievable. For example, they may inform a client that there is a second party partnership that can be created with another company to pull in rich data and that could be used within an audio user interface (AUI) to alert people wearing hearables of a specific offer to a specific audience at a specific time. This subtle but important difference will change the role of the strategist.

Asset Management

The media agency will make many different marketing suggestions, each of which will require assets to be created. Therefore, it will become the unquestioned responsibility of the media agency to establish both a media plan and a specific list of assets – this will include a list of what each agency is responsible for. It will include guidelines on which assets will be created programmatically and which ones will be produced non-programmatically. Agencies that work with global clients will also have to establish which assets will be created centrally versus locally. This will be a new skillset for media agencies.

Investment Planning

Advertisers are increasingly turning to agencies to help them understand how much should be invested in marketing. And this will become increasingly important as the marketing ecosystem becomes more complex. Agencies will offer investment planning, and this will be more than just a specialist service built out from their econometric modelling teams. They will build a capability that will make this skill almost as significant as media planning is today.

Included within this will be an understanding of non-working media costs and also a grasp of long-term marketing investments – using techniques such as NPV (net present value) to enable advertisers to assess marketing investment against other investments that they could make as a business.

New Types of Creatives

The role for creativity will also change. With a large percentage of standard ads being created by AI, the focus will turn towards top funnel brand experiences. New technologies will create remarkable possibilities for brand expression. For instance, brands will be able to create three-dimensional layers that sit on top of the world around us, design immersive virtual reality worlds to replace websites and build cognitive brand characters that have distinct personalities and evolve through interaction. As these opportunities emerge, creative teams are likely to expand and eventually blur into production teams.

The Human Component

These changes in the agency model will force the roles, disciplines and skillsets of current individuals to change. But these individuals will certainly not vanish. There is some emerging evidence that the highest levels of performance are achieved when you pair humans with AI – look, for instance, at how doctors are currently working with IBM's supercomputer, Watson. So, despite these changes, the human component will be very much at the core of the agency: to take the tools, the machines and the technology that have proven useful and add new things on top. The human component will always be to find a better way to improve marketing performance.

ELEVATING

STAGE V

2030 – 2050

Artificial General Intelligence, nano-tech, bio-tech and quantum computing lead to humanity and technology becoming indistinguishable from one another, both virtually and biologically. The Merge is complete. Humanity evolves.

————

As we move into the final – and most dramatic – phase of The Merge, technological capabilities will evolve into the realm of what today we would consider science fiction. Intelligent agents will control whole verticals of business and bots will have automated every administrative process imaginable. Virtual worlds will be as immersive, vivid and authentic as the real thing. And our personal devices, whether they're smart glasses or fitness trackers, will have blended into our bodies.

Much of this progress – says Google's director of engineering, Ray Kurzweil – will be driven by huge advances in the fields of genetics, nanotechnology and robotics. These intertwined revolutions "will transform our frail version 1.0 human bodies into their far more durable and capable version 2.0 counterparts," he wrote in his book, *The Singularity is Near.*

What's more, Kurzweil also believes that machine intelligence will supersede that of human intelligence during Stage V – something he says will be the "most important transformation this century will see. Indeed, it's compatible in importance to the advent of biology itself." And it will take place between 2030 and 2050, propelling our relationship with technology into a whole new stratosphere. Once we've created a machine that can pass the Turing test – which he thinks will

We know what we
are, but know not
what we may be

– William Shakespeare

happen by 2029 – "the succeeding period will be an era of consolidation in which nonbiological intelligence will make rapid gains".

He's not alone in this view. Two scientists called Nick Bostrom and Vincent Müller recently conducted a poll of the world's top AI minds. In the survey, they asked everyone to predict when there was at least a 50 percent possibility of machines reaching "general intelligence" – i.e. becoming as smart or smarter than humans. The average response from these experts was between 2040 and 2050, squarely in the window of Stage V.

This potential breakthrough in AI, complemented by similar advances in nanotechnology and genetics, will underpin the spectacular progress experienced throughout the final 20 years of The Merge. During this period, we'll become indistinguishable from our devices – both physically and metaphorically. We'll be liberated from the biological constraints of our bodies and we'll be elevated to a whole new level – one in which humanity and technology have irreversibly fused together. One in which we've finally merged.

Wearables ➜ Invisibles

The first few years of Stage V will be characterized by the disappearance of physical devices. In Stage III and IV, computers became smaller, more portable and were even attached to our bodies – hearables, for instance, hid a computer inside our ears. But, as we enter the final stage, technology is likely to become even more concealed. Futurologist Dr Ian Pearson believes the smartphone could effectively become an invisible layer of tech on our eyeballs. "If you've still got a smartphone in 2030 you'll be considered a dinosaur," he says. "Augmented reality glasses will completely replace phones, but it won't be long before these are then superseded by AR contact lenses."

In fact, Samsung has already filed a patent in South Korea for a contact lens with an in-built camera, antennae and screen. When developed, this tiny device could let the wearer control an invisible interface with subtle movements, such as the blink of an eye, and therefore replace the need for a pair of glasses or a visor. Google has also experimented with embedding tech into contact lenses. The company's smart lens project, which was announced back in 2014, inserted sensors and a wireless chip into a lens that could monitor glucose levels in tears and communicate that information back to the wearer.

A smart lens makes sense (in theory, at least) because people would be able to seamlessly experience both physical and virtual realities in a completely unobstructed way. But it's also early days in the development process, and other devices will disappear sooner, such as wearables. In Stage III, these (fairly cumbersome) gadgets could extract new kinds of data, like our daily movement and calories burnt. In Stage IV, they became smart enough to predict when we may fall ill. But in Stage V, they will be implanted into our bodies to provide more accurate and useful readings than ever before.

Gadi Amit, a designer who helped create the first Fitbit, is working on a project called Underskin, a tattoo-like circuit board small enough to be inserted under flesh. When developed, he hopes it will be able to track vital signs, such as blood-sugar levels and heartbeat, in much the same way as a wearable device does. Engineers at the University of California, Berkeley, have also created tiny wireless sensors – called "neural dust" – that can be implanted into the body to monitor organ health and muscle development. This dust, which measures 3 mm by 1 mm, can take specific health readings and then send them back to a computer using ultrasound technology.

The medical industry does, of course, already use technological implants in various forms. But most of these – such as pacemakers, cochlear implants and heart valves – are only inserted to treat specific medical conditions. By 2030, "invisibles" will have become much more commonplace consumer products – used by millions or billions of people to monitor health and predict diseases. And inserting them into our bodies will be as simple and socially acceptable as having a dog micro-chipped is today. For many people, the prevention of disease and the elevation of health will be enough of a value-add to balance up the natural resistance to having technology inserted under their skin.

As the fields of nanotechnology and robotics continue to evolve throughout Stage V, invisibles will become even more capable. In particular, the evolution of nanobots – tiny, intelligent machines that can be injected into the human body – will prove to be a game changer. "Billions of nanobots will [soon] travel through the bloodstream in our bodies and brains," added Kurzweil in *The Singularity is Near*. "In our bodies, they will destroy pathogens, correct DNA errors, eliminate toxins and perform many other tasks to enhance our physical well-being."

This may seem like complete science fiction, but there are already a few early signs of it becoming a reality. In 2016, scientists at McGill University, Polytechnique Montréal and the Université de Montréal developed legions of nanobots that could navigate their way through the bloodstream and administer drugs to specific cells in the body. So far, the team has only trialed the tech on mice, but they believe that future developments could provide major breakthroughs in the way we target and treat cancerous cells in humans.

Treatment ➜ Augmentation

Once billions of people start to depend on invisibles, the focus will begin to shift from using them to treat and prevent illness, to employing them to actively improve what nature has given us. "The first entry point is in addressing disease, but the next entry point is going to be enhancement, for sure," says Bryan Johnson, a Silicon Valley CEO.

Johnson's startup, Kernel, is already figuring out this next phase. The company is building devices that can be implanted into the brain to treat neuro-degenerative diseases such as Alzheimer's, and dysfunction such as depression and anxiety. "Our brains are ground zero for everything we are, imagine and create and understanding how to read and write the software running our brains is the most exciting and consequential endeavor in history," he says. "If we are successful in this endeavor, our imaginations fail us in contemplating what will become possible."

The key to unlocking this potential, according to Johnson, lies in understanding our neural code. "Humans are made up of genetic, biological and neurological algorithms," he says. "In genetics, we're increasingly getting better at editing our code to address disease and improve ourselves. The same is true in biology – we've been modifying things like seeds for quite some time. But we haven't yet cracked our neural code, and that's the grand-daddy of them all because in that code lies intelligence – in all its forms – and everything is downstream from intelligence."

If Kernel, or any other company working in this space, can crack the neural code, then a whole new realm of opportunities would emerge. Opportunities that would let humans modify and improve their bodies and minds. For example, a human app store could theoretically materialize where brands could build implants that give people new skills – such as additional memory, more acute hearing or even a higher willingness to exercise or eat the right foods. Could tech companies sell you more short-term memory, much like they do with cloud space today? Or could Skype create a translation prosthetic that automatically deciphers different languages? The company has already built a tool (Skype Translator) that can interpret live speech on its platform, so we can imagine how, over the next two decades, this could be turned into a cerebral bolt-on that enhances our brains.

The Brain-Computer Interface (BCI)

If we can figure out our neural code and design implants that can augment our intelligence, then it's also possible that we could fuse together human intelligence (HI) with artificial intelligence (AI). "This is the most promising area in the expansion of humanity, full stop," says Johnson. "It will enable us to author ourselves and our existence in ways that were previously unimaginable."

Combining HI and AI is no easy task. It would require a giant leap forward in computing power, for starters. IBM is already working on creating the world's first commercial quantum computer, which is due to launch towards the end of 2017. This system, called IMB Q, is designed to process problems and find patterns in quantities of data that are far too big for today's computers to manage. But, as well as supercomputing power, merging HI and AI would also require us to develop a real-time link between the brain and the cloud, so information could flow freely between the two (a bit like how you can Airdrop files from your iPhone to your Mac today).

It's not clear how this link would be created, but tech leaders have suggested some intriguing theories. Elon Musk believes the BCI could be achieved by creating an AI layer that, when inserted into the human body, could act as a wireless transmitter. The Tesla and SpaceX founder announced in March 2017 that he was backing a company called Neuralink, which is reportedly working on an ultra-fine mesh that could be injected into a vein and then, somehow, attach to the brain. "Creating a neural lace is the thing that really matters for humanity to achieve symbiosis with machines," he recently wrote on Twitter.

Facebook is working on a less invasive product that uses optical neural-imaging. They have over 60 scientists and physicists working on an approach that will use tiny cameras that can peer into the brain, using AI to make sense of the data. Their approach measures instantaneous changes in the properties of neurons. Their stated objective is for people to be able to type 100 words per minute straight from their brains – that's six times faster than you are currently doing. Regina Dugan, ex head of DARPA and now Facebook's VP of Engineering and head of their secretive Building 8, announced in April 2017 that this technology is only few years away. Longer-term, Facebook is working on the capability for people to actually share thought – to share semantic information. So you can share deep-thought, independent of language.

Others, including Mark Zuckerberg, Ray Kurzweil and Dr Ian Pearson, believe the BCI could be achieved by sending billions of nanobots into our bodies. As previously described, these bots might soon travel through our bloodstream, administering drugs to specific cells and targeting diseases like cancer. But they could also, potentially, latch on to our brain cells and create a high-speed connection with computers outside the body.

This is even more ambitious that what Facebook is working on. By injecting tiny particles into the brain it will mean that no external apparatus will need to be worn. And science is opening up to this possibility – a team of MIT researchers has created bright, glowing nanoparticles called quantum dots that can be injected into the body, where they emit light at shortwave infrared (SWIR) wavelengths. The next step will be to give them internet access.

"By 2045, we'll have nanotechnology devices connected to every neuron in our brains that will signal their activity to the outside world," says Pearson, "So you'll end up with a replica of your brain running inside a computer, except you can add about 10 zeros to the speed."

Even more startling is the idea that we may soon be able to "rent" additional neurons. Currently, the human brain is limited to around 100 billion neurons and biological restrictions (such as the size of our skulls) mean that it's impossible to expand this. Our memories therefore run at or near capacity and we forget things as quickly as we learn new information. But some futurists believe this will change when we link our brains up to the cloud and obtain access to trillions more neurons – a move that would effectively super-charge our biological brains and give us unlimited memory.

The creation and implementation of this BCI is, of course, still extremely hypothetical. But it's worth thinking for a second about how this kind of invention could impact our lives, beyond greater memory and a higher perspective of reality (if that wasn't enough). Kurzweil, for instance, believes the presence of web-connected nanobots in our brains could let us experience "full immersion virtual reality" that incorporates all of our senses and even our emotions. And we wouldn't have to put on a headset or wear a pair of goggles. Instead, these bots would suppress the inputs coming from our actual senses and replace them with the artificial senses of the intended virtual environment. So, for example, brands could build new worlds (like those explored in Stage III) to immerse the user in, rather than relying on narrative storytelling or hoping the user had the correct device to experience it.

A BCI would also enable us to download new skills or knowledge seamlessly, without the need for cognitive implants. Need to learn a new language for a trip abroad? Want to know more about the history of the Great Pyramids before you visit them? Keen to learn how to play golf? Simple, just download "extension packs" via the cloud and have these automatically hardwired into your brain. Brands could either sponsor or actively enable these exciting developments, therefore being rewarded by consumers for making their lives richer in some way.

Disappearing Devices

A constant, high-speed, wireless connection between our biological brains and the cloud would also rule out the need for an external device – like a smartphone – altogether. "One day, I believe we'll be able to send full rich thoughts to each other directly using technology," wrote Facebook's CEO, Mark Zuckerberg, in a recent post on the platform. "You'll just be able to think of something and your friends will immediately be able to experience it too if you'd like. This would be the ultimate communication technology."

What's more, it looks like Zuckerberg may also be trying to build this future. Facebook's highly secretive Building 8 research lab is currently hiring a BCI engineer and a neural imaging engineer, presumably to work on this idea, or one like it. After all, if brain-to-brain interfacing is "the ultimate communication technology", then it would make sense for Facebook to be exploring it in greater detail.

The creation of this new form of communication will raise as many questions and concerns as opportunities, though. What kind of thoughts could people share? How can they differentiate between public thoughts that can be sent to others and private thoughts that must be kept secret? And, once they've sent it, how can they ensure that they're not interrupting the recipient's own train of thought?

Perhaps it's easier to envisage a world where we could send subtle emotions rather than full thoughts – a world where you could "feel" what your loved ones are experiencing at any given moment in time. Could someone send a "Friday feeling" to their friends via a BCI to show how excited they are about the weekend? Or could a husband let his wife know that's he's thinking about her without the need for anything to be said? This kind of emotional connection – if it were possible – could have the power to link humans together in a collective spirit, and the implications for that could be hugely significant. However, if screens disappear and brain-to-brain communication does take over, what would that mean for advertising? This industry has always relied on interruption, so would ads start to be delivered directly into the brain, interrupting someone's thoughts or emotional state? Will a new industry of super-interruptive pop ups emerge?

Clearly, that feels like a step too far, and there are many subtler solutions that would serve both the brand and the consumer much more effectively. For instance, marketers could pay or position themselves to be front-of-mind (literally) when someone might be most receptive to a particular product. Just like a virtual assistant could call down brands at the right time and place in Stage IV, maybe the BCI will be able to perform a similar function in Stage V. Companies would need to work hard to hand-craft the right associations, as well as bid to be the "thought of choice" when the right impulse arises.

Context would still be key – a marketer's role would be engineering the perfect message for the precise moment in time that someone would be most receptive to it. But this would become increasingly complex, especially as consumers would have the ability to use machine-grade thinking to stress test any brand claims in an instant. There would, in other words, be no gullible or easily-led customers. Brand communications would also have to perfectly reflect the product that it was promoting – any deviation away from that would be picked up immediately by this new breed of "ultra consumers".

Elevated Ideas

This may seem unbelievable, but judging from the rate of exponential progress throughout the first four stages, any advances made in the final 20 years will also be staggering to the people who experience them. "I think that real progress has been made around building technologies that assist, complement and augment human intelligence," says Google's Greg Corrado. "That's what we've built, and that's the direction of things that we'll continue to build."

The brands most likely to succeed in the final two decades of The Merge are the ones that can tap into the intersection of humanity and technology most effectively. This stage requires high levels of experimentation, the development of new skills and an ability to nimbly adapt communication methods in line with scientific breakthroughs. Most of all, it demands an understanding that the future, no matter how hard we try, is almost impossible to accurately predict. As Shakespeare once wrote in his epic tragedy, *Hamlet*: "We know what we are, but know not what we may be." Four hundred years later, as we stand on the cusp of the greatest technological revolution the world might ever witness, those words couldn't be truer.

SUMMARY

In many ways, the world of 2050 feels more like a distant fiction than an impending reality. Brain-to-brain communication, the eradication of disease, nanobots in our bloodstream, our minds linked-up to the cloud. Yet this world is only three decades away. It's a world that many of us will live to experience, and all of us will help to shape.

Of course, some of the specific predictions made in Merge may never come to fruition. Promising early research will flounder, obstacles that we never anticipated will surface and technologies with so much promise will sink into the uncanny valley – never to emerge on the other side. But, before you write off any of the predictions too quickly, just remind yourself of the almost unbelievable progress we have achieved in the last few decades.

If you told anyone living in the 1950s that they'd soon be able to fit the world's knowledge in their pockets, they'd think you were mad. If you showed someone a Facebook News Feed in the 1970s, they'd be utterly perplexed. And if you whipped out an iPhone in the 1990s and ordered an Uber, you'd be considered a wizard. Yet all of these tricks are commonplace today – we do them all the time without batting an eyelid.

Now remind yourself that technological progress is speeding up, not slowing down.

Evidence of exponential advances is everywhere. The telephone took 75 years to reach 50 million users. Radio took 38 years. TV took 13 years. The iPhone took three years. Pokémon Go needed just two weeks.

More than machinery, we need humanity

– Charlie Chaplin

"You're carrying in your pocket a phone that's 100,000 times faster than the computer that sent man to the moon," says Facebook's Sheryl Sandberg. "You're also carrying in your pocket the ability to film a video that would have needed an entire camera crew five years ago."

So, as we look to the future, it's important to remember that what seems like science fiction now – whether it's mixed reality worlds or nanobots in our bloodstream – might just be part of our daily routine within a decade or two. As Mark Zuckerberg wrote in a recent letter to the Facebook community: "We always overestimate what we can do in two years, and we underestimate what we can do in 10 years."

A Bumpy Road

But innovation isn't the only factor that will dictate the future relationship between humanity and technology. A whole range of cultural, political and societal issues must also be taken into consideration. "In theory, there's no reason why most of these incredible advancements cannot happen," says Dr Ian Pearson, "But in practice, our global society is not yet mature enough or constructed in a way to deal with all of this."

What happens, for instance, if an autonomous vehicle runs someone over. Where does the blame lie? With the driver? Or the tech company? And what happens if your VPA overhears a crime being committed. Who is it loyal to – the law, or you? In the US, a case has already emerged where the police have issued a warrant to Amazon asking for audio records from Alexa to be handed over for a first-degree murder trial.

These political and judicial factors are the real unknown. We can chart the evolution of technology pretty accurately. We know that the number of transistors on an integrated circuit will double every two years. We know that processing power will increase year-on-year. And we know that the cost of computing will fall every month. But we can't plan for how society will react to new inventions, or how governments will legislate against them.

And then there are the moral implications. What does this Merge mean for people's everyday lives? Is this future healthy? We're already being warned of the addictive effects of smartphones, for example. "We know that, neurologically speaking, young people are now growing up with an incomplete prefrontal cortex because of this addiction, and we're starting to see other ramifications in the form of anxiety and depression," says Professor Larry Rosen, a psychologist who has studied the damaging effects of technology on humans. Something that, he believes, is likely to get worse as internet access becomes omnipresent. "Augmented realities are going to drag us from a real reality into a virtual world – when you're in this world, you're not truly participating in life."

Perhaps even more challenging are the implications of Stage V. If cerebral bolt-ons catch on, then a two-tiered society could begin to materialize. Wealthy people will be able to alter their genome (to eliminate diseases) and then have their bodies and minds augmented – thus elevating themselves above 'normal' humans. If this happens, then what are the moral and social implications? Do we risk a society that's divided between the 2.0 humans and their lesser 1.0 counterparts – the bots and the have nots?

A Balancing Act

Before we get too caught up with the potential negative impact of tech on our future, it's worth also remembering the incredible good that it can do. "Technology has made us closer together and helped us understand each other, and I think this is just the beginning" says Sandberg. "We find our answers, our resilience and our compassion in a real understanding of who we are as people, and the only way to have that is to gain a real understanding of other people – technology lets us do that."

This is just as well because, barring any catastrophic global event, it's almost impossible to envisage a future where our relationship with tech doesn't deepen significantly. "We live in a multi-nation state globally, where no one country can impose on another its beliefs or adoption of technology and where each country will act in its own self-interest," says Bryan Johnson, the CEO of Kernel. "Because of that, the march towards technological progress will continue and yes, The Merge will be inevitable."

Marketers therefore have a delicate balancing act to achieve over the next two phases of this evolution. They must maximize this opportunity while also taking into consideration the societal and moral implications of progress. Brands must be transparent, honest and always have the consumer's interests at heart. This may seem obvious, but already we're seeing how this equilibrium is being disturbed. Electronics manufacturer Vizio, for example, was recently fined $2.2m for tracking the viewing habits of 11 million households who had bought its connected TV. Vizio captured over 100 billion data points and then sold this information on to advertisers without their customers' knowledge or consent.

A string of other scandals involving smart objects and privacy invasions have also made headlines over the past couple of years. Each one placing a new dent in the willingness that consumers have to embrace technological change. Perhaps this should be expected, considering how important data is to any company's future survival. "Data is the fuel of our future," says Microsoft's Dave Coplin. "AI, ML – the transformational technologies that will fundamentally change almost every aspect of our lives – cannot exist without a plentiful and renewable supply of data."

But there's another ingredient that dictates our ability to collect data – trust. In an ultra-connected era, no trust means no data, no data means no insight, and no insight means no custom. It's as simple as that. So, first and foremost, brands must concentrate on winning the trust of customers while at the same time staying ahead of technological progress. It's a tall order, but one that will increasingly dictate the success or failure of companies in the years to come. As Alan Turing, the father of The Merge, once said: "We can only see a short distance ahead, but we can see plenty there that needs to be done."

REFERENCES

SOURCES USED IN WRITING MERGE

Introduction:
The Human-Technology Merge

Davidson, Jacob, 'Here's How Many Internet Users There Are', Time, 26 May 2015

Goodwin, Richard, 'The History of Mobile Phones From 1973 To 2008: The Handsets That Made it all Happen', Know Your Mobile, 16 November 2016

Johnson, Bryan, interview

Kanellos, Michael, '152,000 Smart Devices Every Minute in 2025: IDC Outlines the Future of Smart Things', Forbes, 3 March 2016

Kurzweil, Ray, 'The Law of Accelerating Returns', Kurzweil AI, 7 March 2001

Murphy, Julia, and Roser, Max, 'Internet', Our World in Data

Stone, Maddie, 'The Trillion Fold Increase in Computing Power, Visualized,' Gizmodo, 24 May 2015

Woodford, Chris, 'A Brief History of Computers', Explain That Stuff, 8 November 2016

Stage I: Surfacing: 1950 – 1995

'Bytelines', Byte Magazine, Volume 6, Number 12, December 1981

Ceruzzi, Paul, 'A History of Modern Computing', The MIT Press, 2003

Chan, Casey, 'This Was the First Banner Ad on the Internet', Gizmodo, 14 February 2013

Chapman, Cameron, 'The History of Computers in a Nutshell', Six Revisions, 21 April 2010

Cook, Carla, 'A Brief History of Online Advertising', Hubspot, 21 September 2016

Copeland, Jack, 'Colossus: The Secrets of Bletchley Park's Codebreaking Computers', Oxford University Press, 2006

Dormehl, Luke, '5 Ways the Macintosh Changed Creativity Forever', Fast Company, 30 January 2014

Gray, Matthew, 'Web Growth Summary', MIT, 2006

'Introducing Apple II', Byte Magazine, Volume 2, Number 6, June 1977

Johnson, Bobbie, 'Apple's Macintosh, 25 Years On', The Guardian, 23 February 2009

Macro, Ashleigh, 'The Mac in Numbers: As Apple Celebrates Macintosh's 30th Birthday, we take a look at the stats', Macworld, 21 January 2014

McCullough, Brian, 'On The 20th Anniversary, an Oral History of the Web's First Banner Ads', Internet History Podcast, 26 October 2014

Murgia, Madhumita, 'The World's First Website Went Online 25 Years Ago Today', The Telegraph, 21 December 2015

Oberoi, Ankit, 'The History of Online Advertising', AdPushup, 3 July 2013

Pruitt, Sarah, 'The Secrets of Ancient Roman Concrete', History, 21 June 2013

Shontell, Alyson, 'Flashback: This is What the First-Ever Website Looked Like', Business Insider, 29 June 2011

'US Digital Display Ad Spending to Surpass Search Ad Spending in 2016', eMarketer, 11 January 2016

Williams, Rhiannon, 'The Early Days of 25 Websites', The Telegraph, 21 December 2015

Woodford, Chris, 'A Brief History of Computers', Explain That Stuff, 8 November 2016

Stage II: Organizing: 1990 – 2015

'Advertising Revenue of Google From 2001 to 2015', Statista

Anderson, Chris, 'The End of Theory: The Data Deluge Makes the Scientific Method Obsolete', Wired, 23 June 2008

Frommer, Daniel, 'How the iPhone Changed Smartphones Forever', 6 June 2011

Gillies, James and Cailliau, Robert, 'How the Web Was Born: The Story of the World Wide Web', Oxford University Press, 2000

'Global 500 2017', Brand Finance, February 2017

'Google Launches Self-Service Advertising Program', Google Press, 23 October 2000

'Internet Users in the World', Internet Live Stats, 5 February 2017

Lasar, Matthew, 'Before Netscape: The forgotten Web browsers of the early 1990s', Ars Technica, 11 October 2011

Markoff, John, and Holson, Laura, 'Apple's Latest Opens a Developers' Playground', The New York Times, 10 July 2008

Marr, Bernard, 'A Brief History of Big Data Everyone Should Read', LinkedIn, 24 February 2015

Marvin, Ginny, 'Google AdWords Turns 15: A Look Back at the Origins of a $60 Billion Business', Search Engine Land, 28 October 2015

McCracken, Harry, 'A Brief History of Windows Sales Figures, 1985-Present', Time, 7 May 2013

'Mobile Cellular Subscriptions', The World Bank

Moren, Dan, 'App Store Tops Three Billion Downloads', Macworld, 5 January 2010

Ng, Alfred, 'Amazon's Best Holiday Season Shipped Over 1 Billion Items', CNET, 27 December 2016

'Number of Smartphone Users Worldwide from 2014 to 2020', Statista

Pavlik, John, and McIntosh, Shawn, 'Converging Media: A New Introduction to Mass Communication', Oxford University Press, 2014

Pintilie, Daniel, 'The History of Web Browsers', Instant Shift, 15 October 2010

Poppick, Susie, '10 Ways Google has Changed the World', Time, 19 August 2014

Rivera, Miriam, 'How Google has Changed the World', Entrepreneur, 29 September 2016

Rosen, Larry, interview

Sandberg, Sheryl, interview

Schmidt, Eric, Techonomy Conference in Lake Tahoe, California, 4 August 2010

Sullivan, Danny, 'What Is Google PageRank? A Guide for Searchers & Webmasters', Search Engine Land, 26 April 2007

'The 1990s Browser Wars Microsoft IE Versus Netscape Navigator', Geek History

'The History of Search Engines', Wordstream

'The Rather Petite Internet of 1995', Pingdom, 31 March 2011

Tibken, Shara, '10 Ways the iPhone Changed Everything', CNET, 7 January 2017

Wegner, Daniel, and Ward, Adrian, 'The Internet has Become the External Hard Drive for our Memories', Scientific American, 1 December 2013

'Windows 95 Sales Plunge from Peak', The New York Times, 8 September 1995

Yanofsky, David, and Mims, Christopher, 'Since 2000, the Number of Mobile Phones in the Developing World has Increased 1700%', Quartz, 2 October 2012

Stage III: Extracting: 2010 – 2025

'2016 Cisco VNI Complete Forecast', Cisco

'80% of Businesses Want Chatbots by 2020', Business Insider, 14 December 2016

Abrash, Michael, Opening Keynote at Oculus Connect 3, 5 October 2016

Adamic, Lada, Burke, Moira, Herdağdelen, Amaç, and Neumann, Dirk, 'Cat People, Dog People', Facebook Research, 7 August 2016

Ariely, Dan, Tweet, 6 January 2013

Bowden, Grace, 'Estée Lauder Launches on Facebook Messenger for One-hour Deliveries', Retail Week, 7 December 2016

Brennan, Dominic, 'Apple Reportedly Could Have Over 1,000 Engineers Working on AR in Israel', Road to VR, 2 March 2017

Bridge, Mark, 'Tracker Badges Leave Workers with no Secrets', The Times, 16 January 2017

Bridge, Mark, 'Woohoo! Amazon's Digital Assistant Gets Excitable', The Times, 14 February 2017

Burn-Murdoch, John, 'Study: Less than 1% of the World's Data is Analysed, Over 80% is Unprotected', The Guardian, 19 December 2012

Campbell, Mikey, 'Rumor: Apple Working with Carl Zeiss on AR Glasses to Debut in 2018', Apple Insider, 9 January 2017

Candela, Joaquin Quiñonero, 'Building Scalable Systems to Understand Content', Facebook Code, 2 February 2017

Chandran, Nyshka, 'Hearables – The Next Big Thing in Wearable Tech', CNBC, 29 December 2014

Constine, Josh, 'Facebook Messenger now Allows Payments in its 30,000 Chat Bots', TechCrunch, 12 September 2016

Coplin, Dave, interview

Corrado, Greg, interview

Dollar, Piotr, 'Learning to Segment', Facebook Research, 25 August 2016

Domingos, Pedro, 'The Master Algorithm, How the Quest for the Ultimate Learning Machine Will Remake our World', Basic Books, 2015

'Ericsson Mobility Report', Ericsson, June 2015

Etherington, Darrell, 'Microsoft to Open Cortana Virtual Assistant to Third-party Devices and Apps', TechCrunch, 13 December 2016

Evans, Benedict, 'Mobile is Eating the World', 9 December 2016

Ewalt, David, 'Inside Magic Leap, the Secretive $4.5 Billion Startup Changing Computing Forever', Forbes, 29 November 2016

'Facebook M Will Begin Making Suggestions in Messenger', Business Insider, 16 December 2016

Fingas, Jon, 'AI is Nearly as Good as Humans at Identifying Skin Cancer', Engadget, 26 January 2017

Franklin-Wallis, Oliver, 'Improbable's SpatialOS is an Operating System for Simulated Cities', Wired, 12 November 2016

Gantz, John, and Reinsel, David, 'The Digital Universe in 2020: Big Data, Bigger Digital Shadows, and Biggest Growth in the Far East,' IDC, December 2012

'Gartner Says 6.4 Billion Connected "Things" Will be in Use in 2016, up 30 Percent from 2015', Gartner, 10 November 2015

Gershgorn, Dave, 'Oxford University's Lip-reading AI is More Accurate than Humans, But Still has a Way to Go', Quartz, 7 November 2016

Gilligan, Andrew, 'Bosses Track You Night and Day with Wearable Gadgets', The Sunday Times, 15 January 2017

'Global Internet of Things Market to Grow to 27 Billion Devices, Generating USD3 Trillion Revenue in 2025', Machina Research, 3 August 2016

Gurman, Mark, and King, Ian, 'Apple Stepping up Plans for Amazon Echo-Style Smart-Home Device', Bloomberg, 23 September 2016

Hilder, Sarah, Harvey, Richard, and Theobald, Barry-John, 'Comparison of Human and Machine-Based Lip-Reading', Auditory-Visual Speech Processing, 10 September 2009

Howard, Laken, 'Nearly One in Three Americans Would Rather Give Up Sex Than Their Smartphone,' Bustle, 20 July 2016

'Improbable Joins Forces with Google to Empower Developers to Build New Online Gaming Experiences', Improbable News, 13 December 2016

'Internet Users in the World', Internet Live Stats, 5 February 2017

Johnson, Khari, 'Amazon Taps Speech Synthesis Smarts to Make Alexa's Voice More Expressive', Venture Beat, 10 February 2017

Kantrowitz, Alex, 'Facebook Tests "M Suggestions", Laying Groundwork for More AI in Messenger', BuzzFeed, 14 December 2016

Kaser, Rachel, 'Amazon Alexa Hits 10,000 Skills with a Nifty Musical Game', The Next Web, 24 February 2017

Kell, John, 'L'Oreal's 'Smart' Hairbrush Wants to Help Solve a Huge Beauty Problem', Fortune, 4 January 2017

Lamkin, Paul, 'Wearable Tech Market to be Worth $34 Billion By 2020', Forbes, 17 February 2016

Levy, Nat, 'Amazon Echo Sales up 9X Compared to Last Year, Company Says in Holiday Roundup', GeekWire, 27 December 2016

Lewis-Kraus, Gideon, 'The Great AI Awakening', The New York Times, 14 December 2016

Majumdar, Anujeet, 'Smartphone Users Check Their Phones an Average of 150 times a Day', Tech 2, 30 May 2013

Mannes, John, 'Facebook's AI Unlocks the Ability to Search Photos by What's in Them', TechCrunch, 2 February 2017

Miller, Paul, 'Google Assistant Will Open up to Developers in December with Actions on Google', The Verge, 4 October 2016

'Mixed Reality Market Expected to Reach $6.9 Billion by 2024: Grand View Research, Inc', PR Newswire, 26 October 2016

Mutchler, Ava, 'Total Number of Amazon Alexa Skills Reaches 7,000', Voicebot, 3 January 2017

'My favourite vending machine', Contagious I/O, 27 February 2014

O'Brien, Chris, 'Facebook Messenger Chief Says Platform's 34,000 Chatbots are Finally Improving User Experience', Venture Beat, 11 November 2016

Odom, Jason, 'Samsung's New Remote Desktop Smartglasses Blur the Line Between Virtual & Augmented Reality', Augmented Reality News, 22 February 2017

'Opening our SpatialOS Alpha, Partnering with Google: Two Big Steps for Improbable', Improbable News, 13 December 2016

Parloff, Roger, 'Why Deep Learning is Suddenly Changing Your Life', Fortune, 28 September 2016

Pearson, Ian, interview

Perez, Sarah, '24.5M Voice-first Devices Expected to Ship this Year, but Apps Struggle to Retain Users', TechCrunch, 24 January 2017

Pichai, Sundar, 'This Year's Founders' Letter', Google Blog, 28 April 2016

Sama, Gabriel, 'Microsoft HoloLens isn't a Toy, Creator Says. At Least Not Yet', CNET, 29 January 2017

Sandberg, Sheryl, interview

Sawers, Paul, 'Hipmunk Embraces Bots with an A.I. Travel Assistant for Facebook Messenger and Slack,' Venture Beat, 23 June 2016

Schroepfer, Mike, 'New Milestones in Artificial Intelligence Research', Facebook Newsroom, 3 November 2015

Schuster, Mike, Johnson, Melvin, and Thorat, Nikhil, 'Zero-Shot Translation with Google's Multilingual Neural Machine Translation System,' Google Research Blog, 22 November 2016

Sentence, Rebecca, 'What Does Meeker's Internet Trends Report Tell us About Voice Search?', Search Engine Watch, 3 June 2016

Shallue, Chris, 'Show and Tell: Image Captioning Open Sourced in TensorFlow', Google Research Blog, 22 September 2016

Sloane, Garett, 'Facebook's New Image-recognition Technology Could be a Data Windfall for Advertisers', Digiday, 7 April 2016

Soper, Taylor, 'Amazon Echo Sales Reach 5M in Two Years, Research Firm Says, as Google Competitor Enters Market', GeekWire, 21 November 2016

Spaull, Simon, 'When 5G and VR Collide', Admap, February 2017

Razani, Amanda, 'Echo Labs Debuts a Wearable Medical Lab on your Wrist', readwrite, 16 February 2017

'Three Million Business Stories', Facebook Business, 2 March 2016

Todorovich, Christine, 'Tech Trends 2017', Frog, December 2016

Vincent, James, 'So, what is Samsung's Bixby AI Assistant Really Made of?', Circuit Breaker, 10 February 2017

Virji, Purna, 'How Voice Search Will Change Digital Marketing — for the Better', Moz, 5 May 2016

Waber, Ben, interview

Young, Wesley, 'The Voice Search Explosion and How it Will Change Local Search', Search Engine Land, 20 June 2016

Zuckerberg, Mark, Facebook post, 9 February 2017

Zuin, Daniela, interview

Stage IV: Anticipating: 2020 – 2035

'Aircraft Passenger Travel Environment Control,' Patent filed by British Airways, 24 March 2014

'Autonomous Cars: The Future is Now', Morgan Stanley, 23 January 2015

'Bitcoin Could Help Cut Power Bills', BBC News, 19 February 2016

Brunker, Mike, 'How Web Search Data Might Help Diagnose Serious Illness Earlier', Microsoft Blog, 7 June 2016

'Computerised Conversation', Contagious I/O, 1 April 2016

Coplin, Dave, interview

Jeffrey, Patrick, 'The Driving Force of Disruption', Contagious, 13 April 2015

Johnson, Kate, 'Sickness-Predicting Wearables', Stylus, 25 January 2017

Kelly, Kevin, 'The Three Breakthroughs that have Finally Unleashed AI on the World', Wired, 27 October 2014

Lomas, Natasha, 'Amazon Patents "Anticipatory" Shipping — To Start Sending Stuff Before You've Bought It', TechCrunch, 18 January 2014

Manyika, James, Chui, Michael, Bughin, Jacques, Dobbs, Richard, Bisson, Peter, and Marrs, Alex, 'Disruptive Technologies: Advances that Will Transform Life, Business and the Global Economy', McKinsey Global Institute, May 2013

Morris, Hugh, 'British Airways Could Serve Passengers 'Digital Pill' to Monitor In-flight Happiness', The Telegraph, 29 November 2016

Paparrizos, John, White, Ryen, and Horvitz, Eric, 'Screening for Pancreatic Adenocarcinoma Using Signals from Web Search Logs: Feasibility Study and Results', Journal of Oncology Practice, August 2016

Patterson, Steven, '"OK Facebook"—why Stop at Assistants? Facebook has Grander Ambitions for Modern AI', Ars Technica, 13 January 2017

'Sensors Enabling a $70B Wearable Technology Market by 2025', Business Wire, 26 August 2015

Snyder, Michael, interview

'The Cost of Sequencing a Human Genome', National Human Genome Research Institute, 6 July 2015

'The Megacity of the Future is Smart', Allianz. com, 30 November 2015

'The Megacity State: The World's Biggest Cities Shaping our Future', Allianz Risk Pulse, November 2015

Thurston, Robin, interview

Turk, Victoria, 'AI Learns to Predict the Future by Watching 2 Million Videos', New Scientist, 28 November 2016

'UN Projects World Population to Reach 8.5 Billion by 2030, Driven by Growth in Developing Countries', UN.org, 29 July 2015

'Volvo Cars of the Future will Talk to Each Other', The Economic Times, 17 October 2016

'Volvo Trucks – New Technology Prevents Accidents by Making Trucks "More Human"', YouTube, 6 October 2014

Vondrick, Carl, interview

Vondrick, Carl, Pirsiavash, Hamed, and Torralba, Antonio, 'Generating Videos with Scene Dynamics', MIT, November 2016

'Wearable Sensors can Tell When you are Getting Sick', Stanford Medicine News Center, 12 January 2017

Wu, Haishan, interview

Zhou, Jingbo, Pei, Hongbin, and Wu, Haishan, 'Early Warning of Human Crowds Based on Query Data from Baidu Map: Analysis Based on Shanghai Stampede', Baidu Research, 22 March 2016

Stage V: Elevating: 2030 – 2050

Bolton, Doug, 'Samsung Patents Design for 'Smart' Augmented Reality Contact Lenses', Independent, March 2016

'Brain-Computer Interface Engineer, Building 8', Facebook job posting

Brown, Kristen, 'Scientists Have Created Tiny Robots that Could Cure Cancer', Fusion, 16 August 2016

Ceruzzi, Paul, 'A History of Modern Computing', The MIT Press, 2003

Corrado, Greg, interview

Diamandis, Peter, 'Ray Kurzweil's Wildest Prediction: Nanobots Will Plug Our Brains into the Web by the 2030s', Singularity Hub, 12 October 2015

Diamandis, Peter, 'The Brain Tech to Merge Humans and AI Is Already Being Developed', Singularity Hub, 5 December 2016

D'Onfro, Jillian, 'Elon Musk Thinks we Need Brain-computers to Avoid Becoming 'House Cats' to Artificial Intelligence', Business Insider, 2 June 2016

Groenheijde, Michel, 'Samsung is Working on Smart Contact Lenses, Patent Filing Reveals', Sam Mobile, April 2016

Hamzelou, Jessica, '$100 Million Project to Make Intelligence-boosting Brain Implant', New Scientist, 20 October 2016

Heath, Alex, 'Facebook has a Mysterious Team Working on Tech That Sounds a lot like Mind Reading', Business Insider, 11 January 2017

Johnson, Bryan, interview

Johnson, Bryan, 'Kernel's Quest to Enhance Human Intelligence', Medium, 20 October 2016

Kurzweil, Ray, The Singularity is Near, Gerald Duckworth & Co Ltd, 2006

'Legions of Nanorobots Target Cancerous Tumours with Precision', McGill Newsroom, 15 August 2016

Medeiros, Joao, 'Gadi Amit Designed the Fitbit, the Lytro Camera and Google's Modular Phone. Now he wants to redesign your body', Wired, 11 September 2015

'Medical Messages', Contagious Magazine, Q3 2016

Meiller, Renee, 'Fast, Stretchy Circuits Could Yield New Wave of Wearable Electronics', University of Wisconsin-Madison, 27 May 2016

Müller, Vincent C., and Bostrom, Nick 'Future Progress in Artificial Intelligence: A Survey of Expert Opinion', Fundamental Issues of Artificial Intelligence

Musk, Elon, Tweet, 4 June 2016

Pearson, Ian, interview

'Reaching 50 Million Users', Visually, 1 May 2012

Sanders, Robert, 'Sprinkling of Neural Dust Opens Door to Electroceuticals', Berkeley News, 3 August 2016

Sonnad, Nikhil, 'How Good is Skype's Instant Translation? We Put it to the Chinese Stress Test', Quartz, 21 October 2015

Zuckerberg, Mark, Facebook post, 30 June 2015

Summary

Coplin, Dave, interview

Devlin, Hannah, 'Kazuo Ishiguro: 'We're Coming Close to the Point Where we can Create People who are Superior to Others', The Guardian, 2 December 2016

Fair, Lesley, 'What Vizio Was Doing Behind the TV Screen', Federal Trade Commission, 6 February 2017

Johnson, Bryan, interview

Pearson, Ian, interview

Rosen, Larry, interview

Sandberg, Sheryl, interview

Steele, Billy, 'Police Seek Amazon Echo Data in Murder Case', Engadget, 27 December 2016

'Vizio to Pay $2.2 Million to FTC, State of New Jersey to Settle Charges It Collected Viewing Histories on 11 Million Smart Televisions without Users' Consent', Federal Trade Commission, 6 February 2017

Wagner, Kurt, and Swisher, Kara, 'Read Mark Zuckerberg's Full 6,000-word Letter on Facebook's Global Ambitions', Recode, 16 February 2017